Another New Normal

Coping and caring for a dog with a degenerative condition

Miriam Valere

This book is published for educational purposes, and is based on the author's first-hand experience. It is not a substitute for the medical advice of veterinarians, or for professional care. Readers should consult a veterinarian on matters relating to the health of their own dogs.

All photographs, unless otherwise credited, are owned and copyrighted by the Author.

ISBN: 978-1-7341107-0-8 (Paperback)

Front cover design by Madison Briggs

Book design and layout by Madison Briggs

Back cover photo by Mischa Safe Dziezyc, ©Dash-D Photography

First paperback printing edition January 2020

Publisher

Aspenglow Publishing
PO Box 522103
Salt Lake City, UT 84152

www.aspenglowpublications.com

Another New Normal

Coping and caring for a dog with a degenerative condition

A portion of all book profits will be donated to the following organizations dedicated to finding a cure for degenerative myelopathy (DM), providing carts for corgis in need, and raising awareness of this disease.

Thank you for helping support these groups!

Dedicated to all the dogs and their loving companions who:

Have taken the DM journey

Are just starting on this path

May your journey be filled with blessings

Contents

Prologue
January 18, 2018

It struck me today that Sassy, my Pembroke Welsh Corgi, can no longer sit up on her haunches. When did I last see her sitting up? Why can't I clearly remember that?

I look through my photos and there it is. *November 23, 2017—almost two months ago.* That was the last photo I have where she was sitting upright. Now she can push her chest up a few inches with her front legs, but she doesn't have the ability to move her torso or hind legs any more.

She looks at me and makes a soft noise—not a whine, and not a bark. More of a "huff," a quiet exhalation of breath that she uses specifically when she wants my attention. She's restless … and I play the guessing game with her. *Are you too hot?* I turn the fan on low, directing it towards her torso. She looks intently at me, and I can see that wasn't what she needed. *Do you need to be moved to a new position?* I turn her over. Still fidgety. *Thirsty?* I move her water bowl closer to her, and she ignores it. *Maybe a potty break?* I pick her up, and put her in her wheeled cart, and then picking up the cart, carry her down the back steps. I pull the cart to help her walk out to the back yard. She's weak enough now that I have to gently pull on the leash attached to the front of her cart to give her the momentum to walk with her front legs. She sniffs a bit, barks at a squirrel, then just stands. I wait. After a few minutes she urinates, and then I express her bowels, and she defecates, too. Soon, I know I'll have to start expressing her bladder. She's now having incontinence to some degree almost daily.

I carry Sassy back to her bed, and get her arranged again. Fresh cooling pad under her. Fan on. Water bowl close enough that she can reach it. She relaxes and starts to drift off to sleep. I sit nearby, working at my computer, and can hear her breathing change. She's asleep.

I have always considered myself to be observant, and wonder why I don't notice things like her not being able to sit up more quickly. I work from home, so I'm with her every day. Other than an occasional errand, such as going to the grocery store, I never leave her side. You would think that these milestones would be seared into my memory.

The insidious nature of the disease that Sassy has, **Degenerative Myelopathy,** is stealing my dog away from me, inch by inch. It happens slowly over the course of many months—the changes subtle to see on a day-to-day basis. Yet when I shift my focus, I can say, *Sassy was able to walk* *on her own on January 1, 2017, and by April 30, 2017 she was using her wheeled cart full time,* or that *On November 23, 2017 Sassy could sit upright, and just two months later, she can no longer do that.* From that perspective, the progress feels rapid.

I'm grateful that I have documented the progressive, degenerative changes that occurred to Sassy through photographs and my journal. The only thing that hasn't changed is her personality. It's like the opposite of dementia—I watched my mother's body remain strong, while her mind slipped away, memory by memory; with Sassy, her mind is strong, but her body is slipping away, limb by limb.

This is her story. Our story. And the story echoed and repeated in a community of people brought together by the love for our dogs, and united by the anguish of a genetic disease called degenerative myelopathy.

Chapter One
Introduction to Degenerative Myelopathy

What is Degenerative Myelopathy?

Degenerative Myelopathy (DM) is a fatal neurodegenerative disease that affects older dogs. It initially results in paralysis of the pelvic limbs but progresses to affect all limbs.

Since first described in 1973 by Damon Averill, DVM, DM has stood for a degeneration of the spinal cord due to an unknown cause. In 2009, a mutation in the gene superoxide dismutase 1 (SOD1) *was described to underlie the cause of DM. Dogs that have two copies (homozygous) of the mutant allele have been shown to be at risk for developing DM. In other words, not all dogs that have the mutation will develop DM so the mutation test is currently a test for risk. Mutations in* SOD1 *are associated with some forms of human amyotrophic lateral sclerosis (ALS), also known as Lou Gehrig's disease, which is adult in onset, causing muscle weakness and eventually respiratory paralysis.*

Degenerative myelopathy is now recognized in many breeds of dogs. Onset of DM is near 9 years of age. In the initial course of the disease, common clinical signs include an asymmetric loss of coordination (ataxia) and spastic weakness in the hind limbs. Owners often report their dogs to be scuffing their nails or toes during walking. In the later stages of the disease, clinical signs progress to paralysis of the hind limbs, urinary and fecal incontinence. Eventually all limbs become weak and swallowing difficulties may also develop. Dogs seem not to show pain during the course of the disease.

Dogs affected with DM often progress to becoming non-ambulatory within 11 months of their initial signs. Due to the difficulties in the nursing care of a large dog, euthanasia is often elected when they become unable to walk.[1]

Those are just medical terms to say the dog you love with all your heart is going to be stolen from you inch by inch, one leg at a time.

That is just scientific terminology to say you're going to become a full-time caregiver to your dog; that you're going to cry from frustration, anger, sadness, and despair over the constantly shifting "new normal" that you have to adjust to. Just when you think you have it figured out, and have a routine that works, something else changes … again. When you think it can't possibly get any harder, it does … again.

And it means that anytime you're out in public with your dog—your best friend and companion—you may hear comments like:

"What's wrong with your dog?"

1. Veterinary Health Center, University of Missouri. "Degenerative Myelopathy." *Facts on Neurologic Diseases.* Accessed on October 15, 2016 through http://vhc.missouri.edu/small-animal-hospital/neurology-neurosurgery/facts-on-neurologic-diseases/degenerative-myelopathy/

Scan these QR codes with your phone for more information.

"That's awful that your dog can't walk anymore."

"Wow, your dog is so spoiled getting to ride in a stroller like that."

And for some reason, these comments from strangers frequently bothered me even more:

"Oh, look how adorable she is in her wheels!"

"That's the cutest thing I've seen all day!"

Those last two comments make it seem like I'm dressing Sassy up for Halloween, like I actually have a choice about her using a wheeled cart. I don't. She's paralyzed, and it's not cute at all.

And then there are the comments directed towards me.

"You are such a saint taking care of your dog that way."

"Wow, you must really love your dog to do that."

I'm not a saint. I'm human, and I'm exhausted. I haven't been away from Sassy for more than three hours in over a year and a half. My entire schedule revolves around her ever-changing needs. She is completely dependent on me.

Of course, I love her. But I'm not doing this for the compliments, kudos, or to prove that I'm a better dog-mom than anyone else. This labor of love is so this bright-eyed, alert dog can still enjoy life until she tells me she's ready run across the Rainbow Bridge, leaving her paralyzed body behind. This book shares the experiences that Sassy and I had during her two-and-a-half-year journey with DM, my feelings about caring for her, and the ways I found to cope with her progressive changes. It is meant to provide a first-hand look at what a DM journey can be like, but is not intended to be a definitive guide on the disease, or a comprehensive how-to book about how to care for a dog with DM. It's important to note that if you are caring for a DM dog, your journey may look vastly different.

While there are many similarities between dogs experiencing DM, there are also many differences. Every dog has its own unique genetic makeup and personality that will factor in how fast the disease progresses, whether secondary illnesses become an issue, and how the dog copes with the challenges of paralysis.

Every person caring for their dog will have individual circumstances that define their DM journey. A single person working outside the home each day will have a vastly different experience than someone, like myself, who works from home, or someone who has a supportive partner or other family members to assist in the care of their dog. If you are elderly, or have mobility issues of your own, you may find that the challenges of a handicapped dog are more than you can safely handle.

Caring for one of the large breeds, such as Chesapeake Bay Retriever, Bernese Mountain Dog, or a German Shepherd with DM versus a smaller breed, like a Pembroke Welsh Corgi (corgi), is also a consideration. Many people are faced with euthanizing their dog when they can no longer use their hind legs, because the physical effort of lifting and carrying a 95 lb. (or larger) dog takes an enormous toll on the caregiver.

Financial resources are another factor in caring for a DM dog as well. If you are living paycheck to paycheck, under-employed, on a fixed income, or unable to work due to your own disability, you will have different decisions to make about the care of your dog.

Don't compare your journey with DM to someone else's and feel you are not doing enough for your dog if you make different decisions in their care, or if you choose to euthanize them at an earlier stage. Each person faced with caring for a DM dog has to decide what they are physically, emotionally, and financially able to handle. As long as you keep your dog active, engaged in your daily activities, and well-loved, you are providing your DM dog with a great life—and that is all that matters to your dog.

Chapter Two
How the troubles began – February 2016

I was walking Sassy (age eleven), and my other corgi, Zeek (age nine), at the park on a sunny Saturday afternoon. We had enjoyed several snow hikes in the canyons over the past couple of months, but today both corgis were enjoying the milder temperatures with bare ground to sniff. We were less than a half block from home when Sassy stopped suddenly, and I saw she was holding up her right hind paw. I checked her pads for stones, stickers, or anything that might be causing her pain, but couldn't find anything. I lightly massaged her leg, and she put it back on the ground and started to walk with a slight limp.

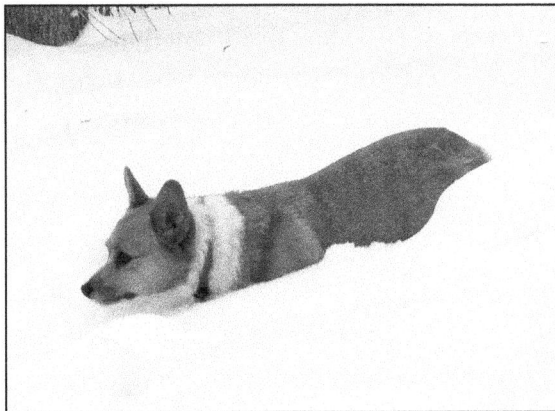

Concerned, I massaged her leg more when we got back to the house, thinking maybe she had stepped in a hole and twisted her leg slightly, or perhaps had a muscle spasm. She was mostly bearing weight, and didn't seem in any particular distress, so I decided to watch her through the weekend rather than rushing her to the emergency after-hours clinic.

Sassy still had a limp on Monday, so I took her to the vet, where they diagnosed a partial tear in her right cranial cruciate ligament (CCL) in her knee (in humans, this is referred to as the anterior cruciate ligament, or ACL, and many vets will refer

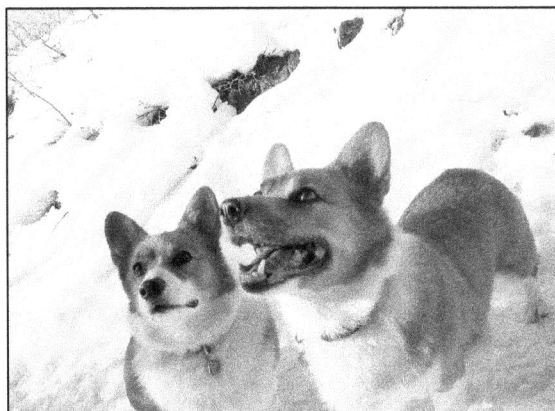

Winter 2016. Sassy (top and above right) and Zeek (above left) enjoyed their hikes in the canyon.

to it in dogs with the same terminology as most people are familiar with that term). The vet took her age into consideration, and because Sassy was able to bear some weight on that leg, he recommended that a conservative approach of crate rest, anti-inflammatory medications for a month, and light activity for an additional twelve weeks would allow her to heal without needing surgery. Light activity meant that Sassy was only permitted to walk as far as needed to pee and poop each day. Of course, we could always revisit the surgery option at a later date if she didn't seem to be healing.

I started to read about CCL injuries in dogs, and confirmed what my vet had said: surgery was not always needed in cases of partial CCL tears in dogs under 35 lbs. of weight, as the body is able to form enough scar tissue around the injury site to hold the knee stable.[2] I felt hopeful that Sassy would make a full recovery and we could avoid surgery.

Twelve weeks of such limited activity felt daunting to me, and I marked the end of that time period with a big red circle around the date on my calendar, and eagerly counted down the days. Surprisingly, Sassy seemed willing to remain quiet, and she was content as long as she was near me. She didn't seem to mind being in her crate when I needed to be out of the house for a couple of hours. I gave her lots of chew toys to keep her mind busy during her forced inactivity. Perhaps being eleven years old was contributing to her willingness to be sedentary.

I figured out a schedule that worked for both Sassy and Zeek. I had to double-up on walk time as Zeek needed more exercise. I would take him out for a long walk, then come back for Sassy and take her out to potty. It was challenging to have one dog in rehabilitation with such limited activity, but I discovered that the one-on-one time with Zeek each day allowed me to continue to work on his impulse control, and he really enjoyed being the center of my attention.

We got through those three months of inactivity with minimal issues, and I was proud of Sassy for handling it so well.

We were heading into springtime, and I was eager to start conditioning Sassy to walk farther distances again. I looked forward to taking her hiking again, as she had always loved spending time in the mountains. For the past three months, Sassy had only walked as far as my neighbor's yard and back, four times per day for potty breaks. I knew from my own experience with having a hip replacement that it's important to build up your strength gradually and not over extend yourself physically and risk a setback. My goal was to have her walk one house farther on my street every two days until she could make it to the end of the block. Sassy was doing great and enjoyed being able to walk more each day. I gave her plenty of time during each short walk to sniff and to roll in the grass. She loved her grass time, and always had the biggest smile on her face as she rolled. We took it slow and easy—no running or jumping allowed—and she patiently listened when I turned her around to go home.

I was thrilled the day we made it to the end of the block. That was a big

2. Puotinen, C. J. (2010). "Alternatives to Surgery for Ligament Injuries in Dogs." *Whole Dog Journal.* Accessed February 22, 2016 through https://www.whole-dog-journal.com/health/alternatives-to-surgery-for-ligament-injuries-in-dogs/

Another New Normal | Miriam Valere

milestone, and I anticipated that I would soon be able to take longer walks with both dogs together.

The third day we made it to the end of the block, Sassy started to limp, this time on her left hind leg. It was exactly twelve weeks into her rehab period, and the vet quickly confirmed that she had a partial tear in her left CCL. My heart sank as I counted out the weeks on the calendar and saw it would be mid-August before she was done with her crate rest/light activity regimen again.

I took Zeek out hiking in the mountains a few times, but felt so guilty leaving Sassy at home by herself that I didn't enjoy the outings like I typically did. Zeek and I continued to take our solo walks in my neighborhood and the nearby park. Sassy seemed quite content, and surprisingly, wasn't all that restless about her continued inactivity. We spent a lot of time outside laying in the grass, enjoying the summer weather. On the weekends, when I had more time, I'd load both corgis in the car, drive to the park, and find a quiet place to sit on the lawn. The dogs enjoyed being able to relax in the grass, nap, and watch the world go by, while I sat with them reading.

As we headed into August, and the end of Sassy's second rehab period was drawing near, I cautiously started to increase her exercise as I had in May, one house at a time. I let her walk slowly, and she stopped to sniff frequently. I watched her carefully to make sure she didn't try to jump or run. I didn't think I could face it if she tore a CCL again; if she did, we'd be dealing with a surgical repair. For a couple of weeks, everything seemed to be back to normal, and I started to mentally relax. I felt certain that she had made a good recovery this time, and these troubles were now over.

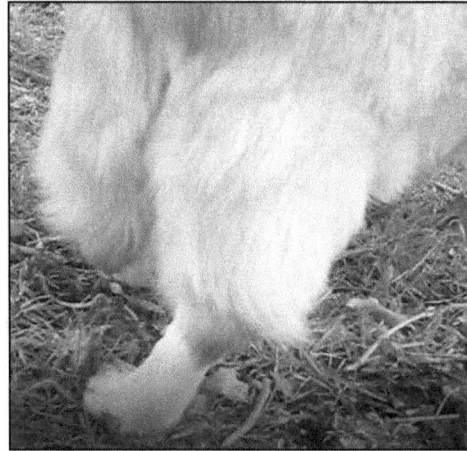

This is what ataxia looks like.

Something is wrong

At the end of the August … this moment is etched into my memory. We had just gone out for our walk, and Sassy stopped to sniff some plants next to the sidewalk. As she was standing there, letting her nose take in all the smells, I noticed that she was not placing her right hind paw correctly. She would take a step, and that leg crossed under her. She was slow to get it in the correct position to take the next step, and seemed completely unaware that anything unusual was occurring with her right hind leg. I felt a clenching fear in the pit of my stomach and knew that something was dreadfully wrong.

A few days later, I heard her toenails scraping on the sidewalk. I checked and the middle two nails on her right hind foot were being worn down. I started to watch her closely for any clues to what was going on. *Was she in pain? Was she limping? What was I seeing?*

I wanted to believe that this was some lingering weakness from her CCL injuries. Every time I would see a misstep, a wobble in her gait, or her right hind paw dragging (referred to as knuckling), I would repeat my mantra: *It's OK, it's just from the CCL. She's fine.* My gut instincts, however, told me that this was something entirely different.

I kept my fears to myself, but became hyper-vigilant in noticing every little difference in her gait. Some days she walked completely normally, and then the next day I'd see something odd. I started to question myself. *Was something really going on? Or was I seeing things?* I constantly sifted through all the symptoms in my mind, hoping that something from my anatomy training from when I was a massage therapist would click into place and give me an explanation for what I was seeing. That background kept whispering *neurological* and so I started my search on the internet. Searches on phrases such as "hind leg weakness in dogs" and "causes of knuckling of paws" led me to several possibilities: *spinal injury, spinal tumor, intervertebral disc disease,* and *degenerative myelopathy.*

My heart sank. *Not degenerative myelopathy. No. That can't be what my sweet girl has.* But some part of me knew it was true.

Learning more

I started to read everything I could about the condition. Most information I found on the internet repeated the same clinical three to four paragraphs about the disease, and the information was as bleak as it was short and to the point: *No treatment options. No cure. Progressive paralysis. Fatal.*

I joined two online DM support groups on Facebook, one for all dog breeds, and the other group was corgi specific. I ordered and read Bobbie Mayer's book, *Corgis on Wheels: Understanding and Caring for the Special Needs of Corgis with Degenerative Myelopathy or Disk Disease.* I quickly learned that Sassy had all the classic early symptoms of DM: weakness in one hind leg only, ataxia (loss of coordination), knuckling with that paw causing her toenails to drag and wear unevenly, and most importantly, no pain.

Her right hind leg seemed to have a mind of its own. When she was standing eating her meals, Sassy would move her body around, but her right hind paw would not reposition itself, so she'd start to lean, or her leg would be at an awkward angle. When walking, that leg would cross under her, sometimes buckling under her. Her toe nails were wearing unevenly from the slight delay in correcting the position of her paw, which caused the top of her toe nails to scrape on the ground.

I massaged Sassy's spine and legs to see if there were any painful areas, and to the best of my ability couldn't see that there were. I watched her closely—dogs are very good at hiding their pain, and Sassy had always been particularly stoic. I didn't see her panting, or any of the other subtle signs of pain. She seemed perfectly normal and happy … she just wobbled when she walked. I knew that wasn't normal.

My mind kept circling back to the words *progressive … paralysis … fatal* and I felt overwhelmed thinking about what it would take to care for a handicapped dog.

DNA testing

I had reached the conclusion that Sassy had DM. I learned from the DM groups that most vets do not have hands-on experience with DM, so I wanted to do my due diligence before taking Sassy to a vet with my concerns. One final step remained—doing the DNA test for DM.

There is an inexpensive DNA test kit that can be ordered from The Orthopedic Foundation for Animals (OFA) (see *Resources*) to determine whether your dog carries the DM gene. The test is a simple cheek swab that is mailed to their lab for analysis.

Two weeks later I had the test results in my email inbox. My stomach clenched when I saw the subject line:

DEGENERATIVE MYELOPATHY RESULTS FOR SASSY.

I hesitated for a couple of minutes before opening the email. My worst fears were confirmed: Sassy was **A/A–At Risk.**

There are three possible results from the DNA test:

- **Normal/Normal (N/N or Clear)**—the dog does not carry the mutated gene at all, and is unlikely to develop DM.
- **Normal/Abnormal (N/A or Carrier)**—the SOD1 mutated gene is on one side of the family, and is unlikely to develop DM, but can pass the gene on to offspring. (Note: there have been some isolated

I am a pet sitter and my first experience with DM happened to a nine-year-old Boxer named Landry that I care for twice a day, five days a week and other times. I had never heard of DM and started researching right away so I could better help her. During this time, her doggy sister died of another disease so I wanted to devote even more time to Landry to help us cope with the loss. Shockingly a few months later, my own Westie was diagnosed with DM. By this time, I was more familiar with DM and noted it seem to happen primarily to Boxers, Shepherds and Corgis. Imagine my utter devastation when my Sammy was diagnosed! I did not even know a Westie could have this condition. Landry is now in end stage and my Sammy in early stage. My heart is broken but I must do the most I can with these two. I have been able to help Landry's mom significantly as being part of a DM group gave me greater insight on how to help my babies. DM is ugly!

—Tammy Diaz
Sammy, West Highland
White Terrier

cases where DM was confirmed in dogs that were a carrier, suggesting that there may be other factors that cause DM to manifest in some breeds.)

- **Abnormal/Abnormal (A/A or Affected/At Risk)**—the SOD1 gene mutation is on both sides of the family, and the dog is considered at risk of developing the disease; but this doesn't actually mean that they WILL develop the disease. Some A/A dogs never develop symptoms.

Presumptive diagnosis

It was time to talk to a vet now. I called Sassy's regular vet to ask if he'd had any experience with DM. He hadn't, and recommended that I take Sassy to Advanced Veterinary Care in Salt Lake City for evaluation. With her results in hand, I took Sassy to the specialist vet clinic to meet with Dr. Morgan. I had a list of questions, starting with did he feel we should do X-rays and an MRI—the recommended testing to rule out spinal issues.

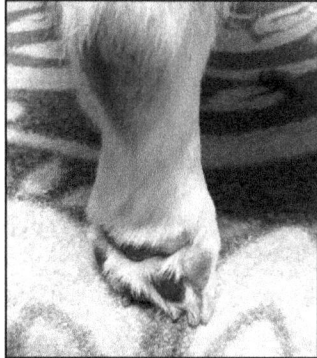

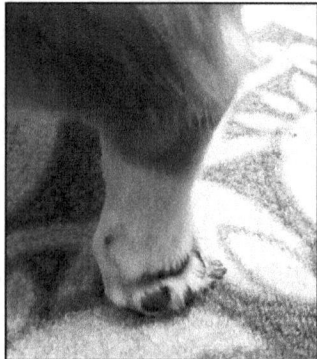

Examples of what knuckling looks like.

Photos credit: Babs Rabenold

Dr. Morgan did a very thorough examination of her back, and did a simple test for her proprioception (the body's ability to sense its location and movements). While she was standing on all fours, he picked up her left hind paw and flipped it so the knuckles were down—Sassy immediately corrected the position of her foot and stood correctly on that paw. He repeated the test with her right hind paw, and the delay before she corrected her paw position was very noticeable. He watched her walk around the exam room, and the loss of coordination was obvious.

As he observed Sassy walking, he told me that he had a DM dog, and was very familiar with the typical early-onset symptoms. He answered all my questions, and felt confident in giving the presumptive diagnosis of DM based on the symptoms she presented with, and the fact she had no obvious pain. He recommended starting hydrotherapy with Sassy as soon as possible instead of spending money on an MRI or other testing. He explained that hydrotherapy was one of the things that can be done to help maintain muscle mass in a DM dog. Muscle atrophy goes hand in hand with DM, so being proactive about exercise will help a DM dog stay active longer.

The challenge with DM is it cannot be definitively diagnosed until the dog dies and the spinal cord is examined under a microscope to see the changes in the myelin surrounding the spinal cord. A *presumptive diagnosis* of DM is given through a process of elimination of other conditions that can mimic the symptoms, such as a spinal injury. Basically, every other disease, injury, or condition that causes similar symptoms is ruled out, so all that is left is DM. Because of the chance for misdiagnosis, it is recommended that any dog suspected of having DM get X-rays of their spine taken along with an MRI, with a neurologist reviewing the results. These tests might reveal that your dog actually has a condition, such as a disc injury in the spine, that can be repaired surgically or treated with medications. It's important to not jump to the conclusion that your dog has DM without additional testing.

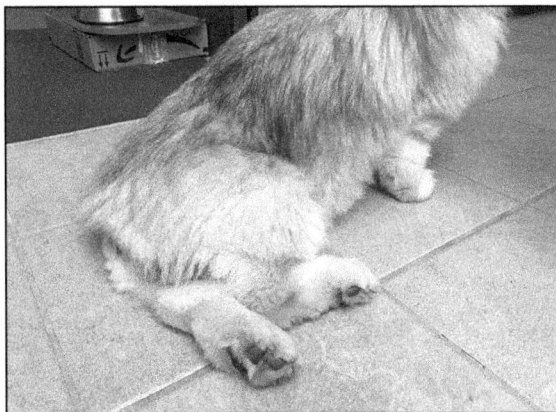

If these tests don't show any obvious issues in the spine, you can be left with a large vet bill, a presumptive DM diagnosis, and no treatment options. MRIs are very expensive, and neurologists may not be available if you live in a smaller community with only basic veterinarian services. Even if these services are available, you may not have the financial means to spend thousands of dollars on tests for your older dog.

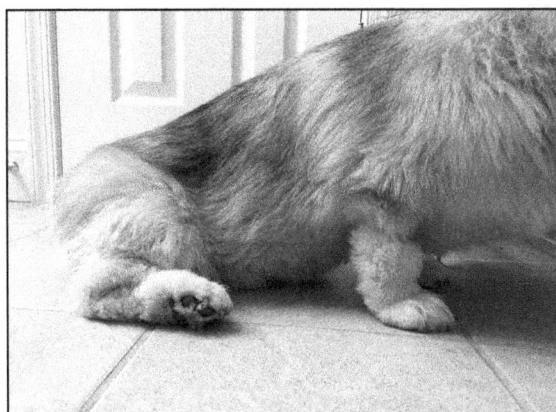

Dogs with DM will frequently sit with their affected leg in odd positions. In these photos, Jasper Islington shows what that can look like.

Photos credit: Joe Harre

I felt fortunate to have found a vet who had personal experience with DM, as many vets have never seen this disease in person. I was able to avoid having additional expensive testing done with Sassy because Dr. Morgan was familiar with the disease, and confident in his diagnosis.

I did have moments of self-doubt and wondered if I should have gotten the MRI. *What if Sassy had something treatable, and I missed the opportunity to care for her properly?* I continued to observe her closely, and over time, felt reassured that she showed no signs of pain or any discomfort. In fact, she seemed to be completely oblivious to the fact that her right hind leg wasn't working correctly. Sassy still had her big smile, and she lived up to her name every day with her spunky attitude.

As we wrapped up 2016, I realized that I had spent almost the entire year in rehabilitation with Sassy. Even though she was free of pain and very happy, I was heartsick to think what 2017 and beyond would bring, now that we had the presumptive diagnosis of DM. I had no idea at that moment just how much this disease would change our lives.

Chapter Three
Starting hydrotherapy

Dr. Morgan had referred me to a local canine physical therapy clinic, Utah Pet Rehab & Acupuncture Center, so I called to get Sassy scheduled for an evaluation. I immediately felt welcomed when we had our first session with Sassy in late January 2017. I was met by the owners of the clinic: Dr. Shawna McCall, veterinarian, and Pat Werner, physical therapist, and together they did a thorough exam of Sassy. They checked her reflexes, tested her range of motion and proprioception. They observed her as she walked around the room, and then worked with her on some exercises designed to maintain her strength and balance that I could do at home with her.

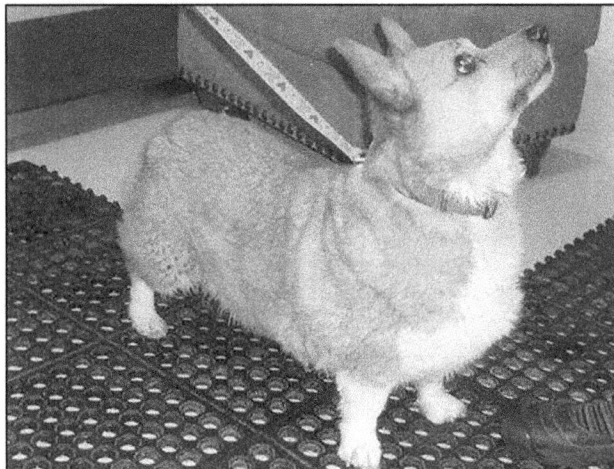

Sassy looking for treats during her physical therapy session.

Pat explained more fully why hydrotherapy was so helpful for DM dogs. Hydrotherapy consists of walking on a treadmill that is submerged in water. Typically, hydrotherapy is considered a rehabilitation tool for a dog recovering from surgery or injury. Being buoyant in the water allows a dog to get exercise without overly stressing joints or an injury site, as the buoyancy reduces the weight of the dog by up to 60 percent, depending on the depth of the water. With a DM dog, the goal is not rehabilitation, as there is no recovery from this disease. The goal is to maintain muscle mass and strength. As DM progresses, the nerve impulses that control movement become interrupted, resulting in muscle weakness, atrophy, and finally paralysis. On land, as the muscles become weaker, the dog simply cannot support its weight on the affected limb, and starts to lose balance and fall. But in the hydrotherapy tank, with the water supporting most of their body weight, the dog can continue to walk fairly normally, even when the hind legs are becoming weak. Additionally, the treadmill movement during hydrotherapy stimulates a spinal reflex that allows a dog with DM to be able to continue to move their affected limbs in water past the point where they could move on their own accord.

While hydrotherapy is very effective for DM dogs, it's not always possible for people to provide this therapy to their dog—either because of the cost, or because there aren't any facilities in their area that provide these services.

Fortunately, walking is also very beneficial for a DM dog, so if you're unable to provide hydrotherapy for your dog, you can still keep your dog active by taking short walks every day to maintain their muscle tone. You can also put PVC pipes or pool noodles on the ground for your dog to step over, or use a wobble (balance) board to help them maintain their core strength, proprioception, and balance.[3]

Sassy in hydrotherapy.

3. Kathmann, I., Cizinauskas, S., Doherr, M. G., Steffen, F., and Jaggy, A. (2006). "Daily Controlled Physiotherapy Increases Survival Time in Dogs with Suspected Degenerative Myelopathy." *J Vet Intern Med* 2006;20:927–932. Accessed May 5, 2019 through http:// dogrehabworks.com/ ResearchArticles/J%20 Vet%20Intern%20 Med%202006.pdf

Because Sassy was at the beginning stages of DM she would benefit from hydrotherapy if she tolerated the therapy. I wasn't sure how this would go, as Sassy had always disliked being in the water—whether in the bathtub, a lake, or a stream. In fact, Sassy typically would balk about taking a walk if it was raining, she so disliked getting wet.

Pat put a flotation vest on Sassy, had her walk up a short ramp to enter into the under-water treadmill tank, closed the door to the tank, and then filled it with ten inches of water. Surprisingly, Sassy didn't fuss or object at all to being on the treadmill, especially when treats were being given to her. As soon as it started to move under her, she started to walk like she did this all the time. She only walked for five minutes the first time—Pat did not want to overdo the exercise and cause Sassy sore muscles.

I felt elated to see Sassy walking so strongly on the treadmill. In the water, I barely noticed any of the ataxia or knuckling that I saw when she walked outside. There was an almost imperceptible delay in the movement of her right hind leg in the water, but anyone not familiar with what had been going on with Sassy would not have noticed it. It was thrilling to see Sassy walking normally again. I also felt a sense of satisfaction that I didn't have to sit helplessly by her side and watch her decline—this was something I could do to help her!

Seeing that Sassy tolerated this first session well, I paid for a package of ten hydrotherapy sessions, and scheduled weekly sessions for Sassy starting the following Saturday. Each week, the Saturday physical therapist, Dr. Tiffany Quilter, would ask how her recovery time was the week before. If I did not notice that Sassy was overly tired from her last session, then Tiffany would increase Sassy's time on the treadmill by a minute or two.

The goal was to have Sassy walk twenty minutes, which would be equivalent to taking a fifty-minute walk on land. Tiffany monitored Sassy closely while she was in the hydrotherapy tank, and her assistant, Lauryn, sat on a bench behind Sassy and made sure that she walked straight ahead on the treadmill, and didn't try to cheat by floating, or not moving her hind legs. Tiffany made notes in Sassy's file about her progress each week, and would sometimes take videos of how she was walking so she could compare month-to-month what changes she was seeing.

Boots, wheel chairs, and assistive devices

Sassy's right hind paw was knuckling often enough now that she was starting to break the skin on the top of her middle two toes. I needed to find some boots that she would tolerate; however, Sassy was one of those dogs that hated having her feet touched or handled in any way. I wasn't looking forward to putting booties on her every time we went outside, or the fight that she would undoubtedly give me.

Tiffany suggested I try the PAWZ booties (see *Resources*)—these booties are more like latex balloons that slip over the foot, and are thin enough that the dog can still "feel" with their paw. At first, I was really clumsy as I figured out how to get the bootie on her paw. It seemed like it should be so simple to pull it over her foot, but Sassy wasn't very cooperative about standing still, and she would pull her leg away from me. But once the bootie was on, Sassy tolerated it well, and it provided the protection that she needed. When the bootie started to get worn out from her dragging her paw, I would throw it away and put a new one on her.

Now that we were five months from first onset of symptoms, it was time to think about getting Sassy a wheeled cart to use. On the recommendations from many people in the DM support groups, I decided to order her cart while she was still able to walk on her own. Wheeled carts (often referred to as a "wheel chair," a "cart," or simply "wheels") consist of rear wheels with side rails that extend up to the dog's shoulders, with a strap or yoke that secures the device to the dog's torso. Between the rear wheels is what is referred to as a "saddle"—two leg rings that the hind legs of the dog are placed in, allowing the dog to stand upright, but fully supported under the pelvis.

This is how the "saddle" looks on an Eddie's Wheels cart.

I think my best tip is that he hated wearing boots so I bought VetRap in bulk and would use cotton wool padding then bandage his feet before every walk. I stressed so much about boots and I wish I'd have thought of the VetRap idea earlier.
—*Carly Lucas*
Kyle, Chesapeake Bay Retriever

Tiffany explained that using a wheeled cart for a dog is similar to a person using a walker or cane after a joint replacement or other injury—it provides stability from falling, allowing the dog to continue to be active for as long as possible. Because of the support a wheeled cart provides, a dog, even with one leg significantly weakened from the progression of DM, would be able to move that weak leg, and not have it buckle under their weight, allowing the dog to continue to use all four legs to walk. When the dog is no longer able to move that leg anymore, there is a "stirrup" that allows the rear leg to be lifted up and supported so the paw isn't dragging on the ground.

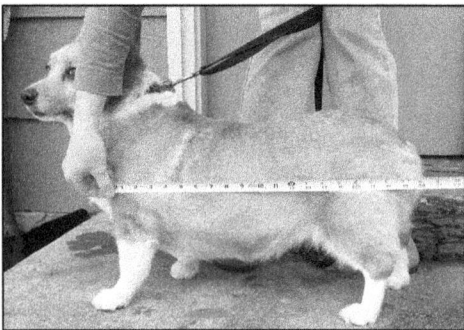

Measuring Sassy for her wheeled cart.

I asked a lot of questions in the groups about the different wheeled carts available, and decided to order Sassy's from Eddie's Wheels (see *Resources*). This brand of cart was supposed to be well-suited for the body build of corgis. Wheeled carts are custom made to each dog's specific height, length, shoulder width, and other measurements. It's much easier to get accurate measurements for the cart size when your dog is still able to stand on its own, which is why I wanted to order Sassy's cart as soon as possible. But even with Sassy still standing, I found it challenging to get the measurements correct, and measured and remeasured her with the help of a friend. I took photos of Sassy standing with a tape measure showing her height and length and hoped that those photos would supplement the measurements I was submitting with my order.

While I was waiting for her cart to arrive, I put down carpet runners and non-skid throw rugs throughout the house. Sassy wasn't able to get very good traction on the wood and tile floors, and she slipped quite a bit. The rugs provided her with some extra stability. My floors looked like a patchwork quilt with a variety of rug colors and designs, as I had picked up several of the rugs at thrift stores to cut down on expenses. I started baking dog treats to sell to my friends in an effort to raise enough money to purchase the cart for Sassy. The expenses were already adding up—hydrotherapy was $55 a session, and her cart was going to be close to $600.

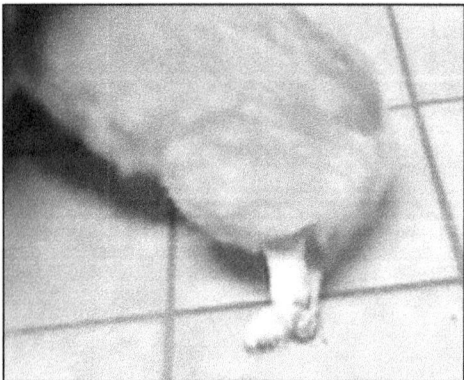

Sassy slipping on the tiled floor.

When Sassy's cart arrived in late February, I got it adjusted for her, then put it in plain view for a week so it wasn't something scary to her. Next, I put Sassy in the cart while she was eating, so she would associate it with something she really enjoyed. I had noticed that Sassy had started to sit when she was eating, as her right hind leg would buckle and give out on her when she was standing. Putting her in her cart allowed her to stand comfortably, and it seemed like she really enjoyed having that freedom to stand and be stable again.

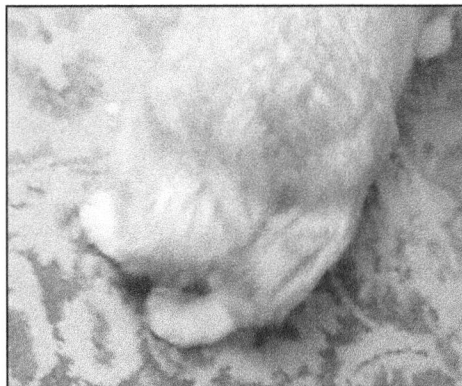

Ataxia is more noticeable now. At this stage, Sassy would frequently fall as her right hind leg gave out under her.

However, whenever Sassy would take a few steps in the kitchen in her cart, she'd fight the cart and pull her back legs out of the saddle. She still had strength in her hind legs and was able to walk on her own, though she did fall frequently as her right hind leg wasn't able to support her weight for very long. I didn't want her to associate her cart with feeling trapped, so I only left her in it for the short time while she was eating.

By March 2017, Sassy was still able to walk on her own, but she staggered in what I called her "drunk sailor" walk. It was heartbreaking for me to see Sassy walking this way, and I became hyper-vigilant to every little deviation from her normal gait. Each small change I saw confirmed how cruel and unfair this disease was.

I lived in a constant state of feeling worried and anxious; this disease was dominating my thoughts. The more I learned about the disease, the more overwhelming it felt. I have always been good with solving problems and getting through tough situations, but the prospects of this disease left me feeling helpless and frustrated. There was nothing I could do that would change the outcome for Sassy, and yet, I had to do whatever I could to keep her strong as long as possible. I knew I needed to figure out some coping strategies quickly if I wanted to be able to care for Sassy and not become an emotional wreck. I reminded myself multiple times per day to *breathe ... in ... out ... relax ... it will be OK.*

Sassy seemed completely unfazed by the changes happening to her. Her new normal wasn't distressing to her at all. At times I found myself feeling very envious that Sassy was oblivious to what was happening to her body. I knew that she would ultimately have the toughest part of this disease, being

KC taught me how to love unconditionally ... how to BELIEVE ... how to pull myself up by my boot straps. I took her out for a walk at the park every day even when I was sick with worry and fear—fear of having to find a way to live without her! She wasn't even gone yet and I was dying inside at the thought of losing her. She would look directly into my eyes and start chatting ... as if to say, "Come on mom! COME ON!" I would ask her if she wanted to go to the park & she would bark (in her faint seal voice) saying "Yes, Yes, YES!" She taught me that we MUST live each moment to its fullest!

— *Tauni Beckmann, #ShadeOutDM, KC, Pembroke Welsh Corgi*

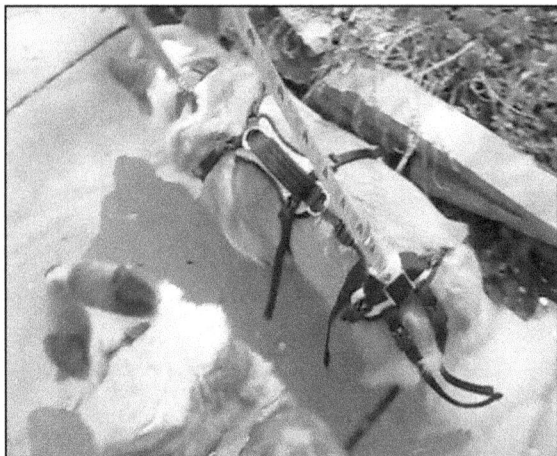

Walking Sassy (with Zeek) with the help of the Help 'Em Up Harness.

in a body that was trapped by paralysis. Living in the moment, as all dogs do, she was unaware of what was to come. I was grateful that if one of us had to have ALS, that it was Sassy, and not me.

By early April, the increasing lack of coordination and lack of strength in her right hind leg was causing Sassy to fall frequently as she walked. The nerve impulses that controlled movement were no longer reaching her leg consistently now. Tiffany suggested that I use a Help 'Em Up® Harness (see *Resources*) during walks so I could support Sassy's back end. The harness fit over her shoulders and hips with a handle at each of those places. I discovered that if I attached a leash to both handles, like a strap on a purse, I could easily walk her and give a gentle lift when I saw her hind leg giving out, which prevented her from falling. I felt like I was handling a marionette as I juggled lifting her back end to keep her walking beside me, with Zeek trotting on my other side.

I'm certain we were quite a sight to anyone passing by as we took our walks every day. Sassy always had an enthusiastic nose for sniffing things, and she was very content to have me hold up her back end with the harness so she could comfortably lean in to smell whatever scent had captured her interest in that moment. Walks evolved from "exercise" to enjoying the time together and taking in the moment. Zeek patiently walked slowly with us, and then when Sassy was tired and back at the house, I'd take him out for a longer walk so he got his much-needed exercise.

Sassy getting used to her wheeled cart. I frequently walked her with her harness until she became fatigued, then put her in her wheels to continue her walk.

By the end of April, I put Sassy in her cart for the majority of our walks. Sometimes I would still use the Help 'Em Up Harness for short potty breaks, but it was getting harder for me to control her movements as her right hind leg became progressively weaker, and she fell more often. In her cart, she still attempted to pull her left hind leg free from the saddle at times, but generally she didn't fight it like she had at first. It was comforting to see how much more stable she was while using her cart, and that she could still move her right hind leg, even if there was little strength remaining in it.

Sassy still had some resistance to using the cart, and she hadn't figured out that she could walk normally in it. She wasn't motivated by chasing a ball, so I knew I had to be consistent with having her use the cart every day, and focused on positive reinforcement. I would take baby steps with her until this became more natural for her. So, mimicking her CCL rehab, we would walk a house or two farther each day as she adjusted to the new routine of using wheels full time. I generally had to lure her with a pocketful of treats, or I would toss a treat several feet in front of her, and she'd run towards it. I rewarded any forward movement with lots of praise and more treats. Some days it felt like I was laying out a trail of breadcrumbs like in the story of Hansel and Gretel.

Sassy was one of those dogs who loved to chase a laser pointer light, or any light reflection she saw. I frequently took her out at night in her cart with a flashlight in hand. I'd shine the light a few feet in front of her, and she'd forget about her cart, and take off to chase the light.

It was a wonderful day when she walked to the end of my street and back, and I felt relieved. I had been trying to ignore my fear that she wouldn't want to walk with her cart. This small accomplishment told me that my fear was just a needless worry, and I could put that one to rest now.

Sometimes she would get really excited if she saw one of my neighbors that she knew well, and she'd take off running in her cart to see them. Those moments made my heart happy. It was a joy to see her moving freely with her wheels. I knew that using a cart would give her more freedom and mobility than she would experience any other way.

When I had free time, I would drive to the park with both dogs so Sassy could have the stimulation of new sights and smells. She was proving she could use the cart really well when she had enough motivation. She became so interested in all the new smells that she quickly forgot about the contraption surrounding her body, and walked easily. Sassy also enjoyed meeting new people, and in the hopes that they might have a treat for her, she would walk up to everyone she saw. It was encouraging to see her walking comfortably in her cart, and it was a much-needed respite from the worry I had been carrying for so many months about her decreasing mobility. I celebrated every little achievement she made during this time.

My Rookie, a female GS, was diagnosed with DM in January 2019. She can still walk but her legs get twisted and she falls on slippery floors. In the beginning I had to learn to hide my feelings when this happened. I would gasp and cringe when it happened and I soon realized that my gasping scared her more than the actual sliding and falling. We put down a lot of rugs on our tile floors which helped immensely. She has now learned to walk on the rugs and bypasses any open spots of tile flooring. Dogs are so smart. Rookie has adjusted well to each stage of this horrible disease so far … I am the one who has a hard time—it breaks my heart to watch her but I do my best to stay positive especially when I am around her. She gets lots of love and treats and will continue to do so until it is her time to go to the Rainbow Bridge.

—*Rookie's mom*
German Shepherd

I also celebrated similar victories in the DM support groups. People posted questions about how to cope with certain facets of having a DM dog, or to vent their frustrations, fears, and worry. But they also posted family vacation photos of their DM dog happily playing on the beach using her wheels, or chasing after a squirrel, or being so enthusiastic about running that he tipped his cart over. The sheer joy and exuberance of those photos buoyed my spirits, and I started to slowly shift my thinking. *Perhaps there is life after a DM diagnosis. Perhaps we can still find joy together.*

Chapter Four
Seal walking and other changes

As Sassy's right hind leg became even weaker, she could no longer support her weight when standing unassisted. This change resulted in what is referred to as "seal walking." A DM dog will be in a sitting position and pushes off with the strong hind leg, pulling their body with their front legs, which causes the dog to scoot on their haunches. Sassy was surprisingly fast navigating in the house that way, and could quickly follow me from room to room with no difficulties. If this change in her mobility bothered her in any way, she certainly didn't let me know. She could still chase after my cats while she was seal walking, and that made her happy. I used to scold her for chasing the cats, but now I found myself encouraging her to do that. I didn't want her to lose her spunky attitude and become depressed. My cats had plenty of places to hide from the dogs, so I think it was a game they all liked to play with Sassy.

Sassy in seal walking position. She could pull herself with her front legs, and push with her left hind leg.

It was also around this time that Sassy's bark changed from the deep, big bark she always had, to a hoarse sounding "seal" bark. Many people who have had a DM dog are familiar with the sound of the "DM bark"— it is very distinctive, and is thought to be the result of the nerve input to the diaphragm not working correctly anymore. Some DM dogs will have a "breathy" or "airy" quality to their bark instead of developing the "seal" bark.

Another big change that occurred during this time period was in the pecking order of my dogs. To explain the significance of this, I need to explain the background (and baggage) that Sassy and Zeek came with.

Sassy probably should have been an only dog. She had always been a strong alpha and barely tolerated having any other dogs around her. If she saw a dog on the other side of the street when we were outside, she'd growl. She wasn't having any of that nonsense of playing and jumping around, or being even remotely social with other dogs. I referred to her as the "fun police." It wasn't that she was aggressive with other dogs; she just did not tolerate having them in her space. She definitely was more people-oriented than dog-oriented. When I used to take her to our local corgi meet-ups, she would ignore all the dogs—or growl at them, frequently baring her teeth—and focus intently on the people, especially if they had their hands in their pockets. That was her cue that there were treats hidden in those pockets, and she would sit at that person's feet and look her most charming until they would give her a treat. If a treat wasn't forthcoming, she would find her next victim and shamelessly work the crowd for treats.

Sassy's relationship with Zeek was complicated. Sassy, and then Zeek, had been originally rescued by a member of my family. When Tina's life took an unexpected detour, and she found herself in the middle of a divorce without a job in late summer of 2015, she asked me if I would take the dogs until she could get back on her feet. I had recently adopted Lexx, a senior corgi with lung cancer, and wasn't sure I could handle taking care of three dogs. But I knew Lexx wouldn't be with me much longer, so reluctantly, I agreed to take on Sassy and Zeek.

From 2015, Sassy, Zeek, and Lexx.

When I first took on responsibility for the dogs, both were extremely stressed, and they fought with each other seven to ten times per day—and not just with growls and posturing. They had full-blown fights, and I was ill-prepared to handle this. The level of aggression between them was a huge challenge for me, as I was a novice when it came to this kind of dog behavior; the few dogs I'd had previously in my life were sweet, well-mannered, mellow dogs. Fights would erupt daily during walks when something triggered Zeek, and he would misdirect and attack Sassy. She would defend herself, and the attacks quickly spun out of control.

In the house, tensions would flare up with no obvious trigger that I could see. One moment, all seemed calm, and then Zeek would lunge and be at Sassy's throat in a split second. Had Sassy been docile and submissive, the fights would have de-escalated quickly, but she was anything but that. The minute Zeek would attack her, she would unleash her fury on him, and nothing would make her back down. The times when blood was drawn during a fight only seemed to make Sassy that much more determined to put Zeek in his place. When they were both triggered like this, neither one would respond to any voice commands, so I had to physically pull them apart with all my strength, and pray I didn't get bit too often in the process. The first week I had them, I pulled them apart so many times that my hands were in intense pain from grabbing them by the scruff of their necks and the effort of physically restraining them. I knew that physically dominating them wasn't the answer, but I didn't know what else to do in that moment. I questioned my sanity to take on these dogs, but was determined to find a solution to their behavior issues.

This was an unhealthy situation for all of us. I frequently separated them in different rooms to lower the tension levels, or gave them both time in their crates to decompress. I learned to pay close attention to what their triggers were, and worked on some pattern interrupts to modify their behavior. Zeek had strong herding instincts, plus a high prey drive, so his triggers were frequently things like a dog running off leash, or chasing a ball. He either wanted to herd it or catch it, and became very frustrated when he couldn't. Zeek also had a strong dislike for smaller dogs, and would lunge aggressively if any walked near us. We stopped attending the corgi meet-ups after Zeek saw a puppy half-way across the field, and ran full-speed to attack it. Fortunately, the person who had the puppy was able to scoop him up quickly, and no physical damage was done. But this level of aggression was an issue that had to be dealt with. We lived very close to a dog park, and there were always people walking their dogs when we were out. I couldn't avoid every dog, and had to figure out how to modify this behavior.

Fortunately, both Zeek and Sassy were highly food motivated, so whenever

From 2015, Sassy and Zeek in full begging mode.

I saw something that I thought would be a trigger when we were walking, I took a treat out of my pocket and asked them both to sit, and they looked at me until the "threat" had passed. I'd reward that positive behavior with a lot of praise and the treats, and that simple technique started to make a huge difference. There were noticeably fewer fights while we were walking, but we still had a long way to go.

After Lexx died in October 2015 after just six short months together, I was devastated. He was such a good dog, and I wanted so much more time with him. By now, I realized that emotions were a big trigger for Zeek, so I had to keep my grief about losing Lexx guarded as much as possible so I didn't upset the dogs even more.

I needed more insights into their behavior and decided to consult with an animal communicator. I know that many people think animal communication is a bit far-fetched, but I have always believed that all creatures are sentient. Just because animals can't use human speech, doesn't mean they aren't talking to us! If we can open our hearts and our minds, we can sometimes "hear" what they have to say. But I also knew that sometimes my own bias would get in the way, and I either would not "hear" the message clearly, or I would second-guess myself on what that message was telling me. With the complex issues I had with Zeek, and the dynamic with Sassy, I thought an animal communicator might be able to get to the heart of the problems.

I asked around for a good communicator, and was given Valerie's name. I called her to schedule an appointment, and hoped that she would be able to provide some insights. Our first conversation was very revealing. Valerie told me that Zeek had a lot of anxiety and fear, and that he was afraid that I wasn't going to keep him. She told me that he was like a young child who really needed security and constant reassurance. On the other hand, Sassy was like a teen-ager: cocky, strong-willed, and sure of herself. Sassy was confident that she would never live anywhere else but with me—a statement that I questioned, because Tina had repeatedly told me that as soon as she was settled and could afford it, she wanted to take Sassy back. I told Valerie that, and she asked Sassy for clarification. Sassy's response was direct and to the point: *Don't worry about it, I'm always going to live with you.* Valerie's insights into both of their emotional states was helpful, and she encouraged me to continue to be very consistent, give the dogs plenty of walks, and reward positive behavior.

Another clue in unraveling their issues came in an unexpected way. I had made a post about Zeek's behavior in the Utah Corgis Facebook group, and asked for tips to help defuse his aggression, especially directed at smaller dogs. A woman I didn't know replied that Zeek didn't like small dogs. I contacted her privately, and asked her what she knew about Zeek's background, only to find out that Zeek came from their kennel! I quickly arranged a call with her to see if I could piece together his background. Tina had been told about Zeek being in another home prior to the family she adopted him from, and now talking with his breeder, I found out that Zeek had been placed once, then returned to them, placed again, and then they had lost track of him and had no idea where he was until they saw my post. By my count, that meant that Zeek had now been in a minimum of seven homes—and he was only eight years old! No wonder he had some major anxiety and was afraid I wasn't going to keep him!

At this point, I invested in one-on-one dog training sessions for Zeek to learn how to handle him better, as he surely had some deep-seated behavioral issues causing his aggression. Those sessions with the trainer were eye-opening, and I learned so much about dog behavior, and how to better work with Zeek.

Over time, Zeek's behavior slowly improved, and he didn't attack Sassy as often. I was able to have them in the same room together and didn't need to separate them all the time. But with Sassy losing the use of one hind leg, I was really concerned that Zeek would attack her as he had in the past, and that Sassy wouldn't be able to defend herself as easily. That scenario could end badly if Zeek injured her. As a precaution, whenever I left the house to do errands, I made sure to put Zeek in another room or in his crate.

Proof of the change in dynamic in the pack: Sassy and Zeek sleeping close to each other.

So, it was with great surprise in late March 2017 when I noticed that Sassy and Zeek were tolerating each other better. Fights were greatly reduced—in large part due to the training I had done with Zeek—but there was also a noticeable shift in the energy in the household. In the evenings Zeek would be stretched out sleeping close to Sassy, something that never had happened before. They seemed to have declared a truce, and while Sassy still maintained a certain level of authority in the household, it looked like perhaps she had willingly turned over the alpha role to Zeek.

Chapter Five
The normalcy of disability

As May 2017 ended and we headed into June, Sassy was using her cart all the time now. She seal walked around the house anytime she wasn't in her cart. We continued with her weekly hydrotherapy sessions and she was able to walk on the underwater treadmill for 15–18 minutes at a time now. The weakness in her right hind leg continued to progress, but in the water, she still had movement of that leg.

I felt more comfortable with my role of caregiver for a disabled dog. We had a routine that worked well on most days. While Tiffany had not been able to find a canine physical therapy study specifically for DM, she extrapolated from human ALS studies that five ten-minute walks were more beneficial than one 50-minute walk a day, so I made sure Sassy got out every day for several short walks. Working from home allowed me to be flexible with my schedule so I could more easily accommodate Sassy's needs.

Zeek was surprisingly patient with Sassy, and would sit and wait for her to catch up when we were out walking. It was a relief to see how much better he was interacting with her.

Our summer was uneventful, and as August approached marking Sassy's one-year anniversary of first onset of symptoms, I breathed a sigh of relief. Sassy was enjoying our trips to the mountains for short hikes, and ongoing visits to the park. She had accepted using her cart really well, and her feisty, determined attitude was evident at all times. She seemed to enjoy her weekly hydrotherapy sessions, and true to form, she loved all the treats and attention she received during those appointments.

Sassy enjoying a little hike in the mountains. Notice how her hind legs are both at an angle. As she became weaker in her hind legs, she leaned on them like this.

I typically didn't leave Sassy in her cart when she was in the house, but I would if it was right before meal time, since she needed to use her cart while she ate. It was endearing to see how she would wheel herself into the living room after she ate her meal, and take a nap in her cart. She would rest her head and front legs on the floor, which caused her cart to tilt forward, putting her back end up in the air. She seemed to be very comfortable in that position,

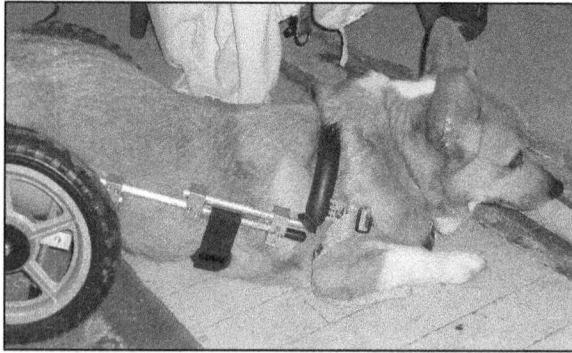

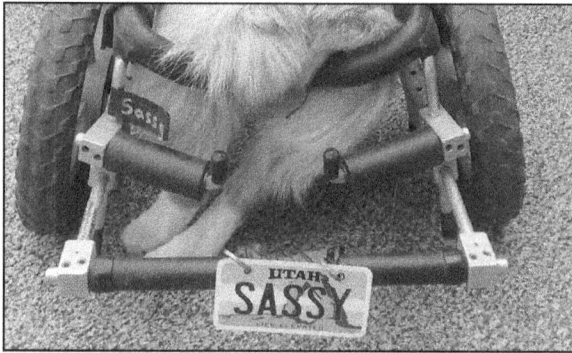

Top, Sassy getting ready for a nap in her wheels. Above, showing how her right leg was becoming extremely weak and unable to move correctly.

but when I saw she was ready to lie down, I felt she would rest better if she could stretch out on the floor or her bed, so I'd take her out of her cart.

At night, after her bedtime potty break, I left Sassy in her cart, and she quickly learned to wheel herself down the hallway, and stood in front of her bed, where she patiently waited for me to take her out of her cart and tuck her into bed. That became our nightly ritual, and I cherished that tender moment each night with her. She tolerated me picking her up, getting her settled into bed, and even allowed me to give her a kiss on the top of her head as I told her goodnight.

This disease that I had originally feared and dreaded wasn't as difficult as I had imagined it to be. I had to do things a little differently with a dog in wheels, but it was manageable. I was finding a routine that worked for both Sassy and Zeek's particular needs, and feeling more confident in my ability to care for Sassy.

Fall 2017

Sassy remained strong in hydrotherapy, though it was obvious that her right

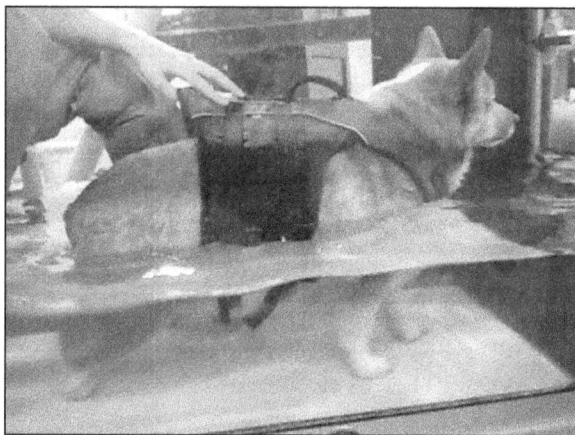

You can see that her right hind foot is turned in during hydrotherapy. The disease is advancing.

hind leg was getting progressively weaker. I took weekly videos of her walking in hydrotherapy so I could compare from week-to-week what changes I was seeing. Tiffany continued to be encouraged about her strength, and felt for a dog who was one-year post-onset of symptoms that Sassy was doing great. Many DM dogs lose the use of their hind legs by the one-year mark, so I was hopeful that between our multiple daily walks and the weekly hydrotherapy, that Sassy would remain active for many more months. I knew we weren't able to stop the disease from progressing, but maybe her therapy would allow her to stay strong for a longer time.

Another New Normal | Miriam Valere

Sassy loved being outside taking naps. I felt it was important to give her plenty of fresh air and time to just "be a dog."

I felt optimistic that Sassy had several months of walking in her cart ahead of her. I started to anticipate snow season, and had seen videos of handicapped dogs using wheeled carts with a ski attachment. That looked fun, and I knew that both my dogs would enjoy a good romp in the snow.

Tilly was diagnosed with DM in May 2016, and I've had a lot of time to reflect over the nearly three years we have been living with this disease. The most important thing I have done throughout this journey is to never treat Tilly like she is disabled, or incapable of enjoying life. Our daily routines may have changed as the disease has progressed, but Tilly's spirit has not—she is just as loud, stubborn, and full of zest as she ever was! She loves car rides, trips to the park, and yelling at me for her breakfast just as much as she did when she had her mobility. Just because this disease has robbed her of her legs does not mean she cannot live her life with me to the fullest. Tilly's spark is alive and well, and I try to remind myself of that when we are having our toughest days. I would not trade this journey with her for the world.

—*Kirsten Nuffer*
Tilly,
Pembroke Welsh Corgi

Chapter Six
And then we were three

In early October 2017, I adopted a senior corgi named Frodo who was being rehomed. I knew that adding a third dog would change the dynamics of the household, and I anticipated having a "pair and a spare" scenario. I assumed my "pair" would be Sassy and Frodo, as I thought with Frodo being almost fifteen, he wouldn't be as active as Zeek. But I was wrong. Zeek and Frodo quickly decided they enjoyed walking together, so they became my "pair," and Sassy was my "spare."

The newest member of the family, Frodo.

The logistics of walking three dogs, one in wheels, took some coordination on my part. In the mornings, I would walk Zeek and Frodo together while Sassy slept in, then would take her for a short walk in her cart before breakfast. At lunchtime, all the dogs had free time in the back yard, and Sassy would walk around some, but mostly seemed content for a quick midday potty break. After work, I would take Sassy out by herself for her short walk, and then put her back in the house, and turn around immediately to take the boys out for a longer walk. I would repeat that routine at bedtime with a slightly shorter walk—but it felt like all I was doing was walking dogs during every free moment.

I wanted to be able to take the dogs out together for longer walks, but of course, Sassy wasn't able to walk the same distance, or at the same speed that the boys could. I decided the best solution was to buy a wagon to pull Sassy in.

Walking the boys with Sassy going for a ride.

I loaded Sassy in the wagon, tied her cart to the back of it, and pulled her while walking Zeek and Frodo. Sometimes, to free up my hands, I would tie Frodo's leash to the wagon and he walked right behind it. When we got to the park, I put Sassy in her cart to let her get some exercise, and to smell all the delicious scents she could find.

The wagon was collapsible, so when I was off work, I'd load the dogs in the car, along with Sassy's wagon and cart, and we'd go exploring. The act of loading all of Sassy's gear in the car, and getting three dogs in the car, reminded me of getting several small children ready to go someplace—I felt like I had triplets. But the extra work was worth it as all three dogs loved the outings to different parks, and I could see the mental stimulation was good for Sassy.

We made leaf piles to play in, and I made a point of taking many photos of all the dogs, but especially of Sassy. I think autumn was Sassy's favorite season, because she was so playful in the leaves. She would bury her head in the leaves, and toss them with her nose. Her beautiful brown eyes sparkled and she was filled with delight from being out in the crisp fall weather. It made me happy to see her rolling in the leaves and being playful.

Sassy enjoying the autumn leaves.

Frodo was a sweet, docile old gentleman. He had been neglected for most of his life, and hadn't received any kind of vet care. He acted very grateful to be in a comfortable home, to have a soft bed to sleep on, and to be loved. He spent most of his time near Zeek, and seemed to enjoy being part of a pack. Based on what Frodo's previous owner had told me, I felt that Frodo had rarely experienced the kind of activities I liked to do with my dogs. I was determined to pack as much fun into our routine as I could—to make up for lost time for Frodo, and to make sure that Sassy got to enjoy her life as much as she could with the limitations this disease put on her.

My wagon full of love.

Frodo did not have an assertive bone in his body, and yet Sassy felt it was her job to remind him who was in charge. If he walked by her when she was in her cart, she would lunge and try to nip his rump. He'd be so startled that he'd jump out of the way and hide behind my legs. When I would see her do that, I'd just shake my head and remind myself that she was living up to her name once again. If there was ever a dog whose name represented their personality perfectly, it was Sassy.

Another New Normal | Miriam Valere

Chapter Seven
Setting thresholds

With DM comes the heartbreaking awareness of what lies ahead. While the speed of the progression of the disease is unique with each dog, if a dog lives long enough with the disease, it is possible that many of these milestones or thresholds may be reached at some point:

- Loss of use of the first hind leg affected
- Seal walking
- Weakness and loss of proprioception in other hind leg
- Muscle atrophy in hind legs, hips, and along the spine
- Being completely "down" in the back (loss of use in both hind legs)
- Incontinence (bowels and/or urinary)
- Weakness in the front legs
- Being completely down (front and back)
- Respiratory issues

At the beginning, when I was first learning about this disease, it was easy to look ahead and say, *When Sassy reaches [fill in the blank stage], I will let her go.* I was certain at the time that she would not be happy at that point, and I was equally certain that I wouldn't be able to cope with that stage. I saw similar comments frequently on the DM support groups, as everyone struggled to come to terms with this disease. I suspect that this tendency to attempt to set a threshold was part of the anticipatory grief that goes hand in hand with a diagnosis of a degenerative, progressive disease. We attempt to buffer our feelings to somehow soften the blow of the steady decline that we know is coming. Perhaps it was a way of feeling more in control while everything around you was spinning rapidly out of control.

As Sassy reached each new stage, my first reaction was always *This is so awful* ... and then a few months later, looking back, I would give anything if I could go back to that previous stage. I remember how horrified I felt watching Sassy walk when she first started her "drunk sailor" stage. It broke my heart to see her staggering and falling so much when she walked, and I was fixated on how unfair and awful this loss of coordination was. Yet it didn't upset Sassy at all, and it certainly didn't stop her from going where she wanted to go. She would stumble and fall, and then get up and keep

Setting thresholds. Many of us here have done this and changed it many times. I then learned not to even do that. It's hard and so much was unknown. I was "sure" early on that I knew what both us and our boy could handle. I was never more wrong. Just take one day at a time and maybe you'll pass right by that threshold, as others have before you, and maybe you won't, but you really won't know until you are there. I would say try not to think too far in the future—it keeps us from living in the now—which is how our dogs live. They live each day and don't worry for the future. Once I learned to really live that way the journey got easier.

—Pam Barnes
Loki, German Shepherd

Sassy may not be able to walk without assistance, but she's still a happy pup.

When my wife and I first received Jasper Islington's presumed diagnosis of DM we were devastated and overwhelmed. While the devastation will never change, what has been critical for us is focusing on the present. We all know how this ends and dwelling on it does nothing but hurt. Instead we think only of right now: Just for today, Jasper Islington is comfortable, smiling, and able to get around all by himself. Today is what is most important. We will not mourn what has been lost, but celebrate what we still have. That is easier said than done, but it helps us immeasurably.

—*Jasper Islington's Mum and Da, Pembroke Welsh Corgi*

walking. Occasionally she looked confused for a split second, but I'd help her up, and she quickly forgot that she had fallen.

What I discovered in the relatively slow progression of this disease was Sassy adapted, and so did I. Whatever those "milestones" were that I imagined would be so awful weren't that bad once I got used to the "new normal." I found out as we arrived at each different stage, that Sassy was still happy, engaged, and enthusiastic about life. So, I simply adjusted to yet another new normal from this debilitating disease.

When it came to drawing some imaginary line in the sand and saying, *My dog will be so unhappy when [fill in the blank] happens, and I won't be able to cope,* we think we know our dog and ourselves, but most of the time we're wrong. The changes occur slowly, giving you time to find what works for you and your dog—or even more likely, you've simply been responding each day to the smallest of changes without even realizing that you started to do things differently. That threshold arrives and you realize you have adapted. You discover it's not nearly as hard as you thought it would be. And your dog is still happy, so why would you give up now?

Staying present

What I was starting to learn from caring for Sassy was to stay focused on the present. Dogs live in the moment—it's one of the qualities that I love the most about animals. Being fully present for whatever is happening to them in this moment, dogs embrace life with enthusiasm. Small children frequently exhibit this same joyful abandon, but as adults, we are too distracted by what we need to do next, earning a living, our worries about tomorrow, and our fears that hold us back. All of those distractions prevent us from simply appreciating the moment we're in.

Sassy was a master of this gift that all animals have. She lived in the "now" at each moment of her life. Without the ability to compare her current "now" with what she had last week, she was able to live full of grace and dignity, even while this disease ravaged her body and slowly paralyzed her.

Being the caregiver of a disabled dog, it was easy to get lost in worry about tomorrow. The first several months of walking this path with Sassy,

I grappled with coming to terms with the prognosis of this disease—and that stole away the joy of the moment. When I look back on that time period when Sassy was still able to be mobile on her own, it makes me sad; I was so immersed in projecting ahead about what was to come, that I lost those precious days of appreciating what she was still easily doing. But I also learned there was no point in regretting what I didn't know how to do at the time.

In the early stages of her disease, I focused on learning what this disease was all about. I was getting acquainted with others in the corgi community who had gone through this before, or were currently going through it, as I knew I needed their support and guidance. I can't go back in time and relive those early days—but I could take that feeling of regret, and of missed opportunities and apply it to my present moment, and strive to do better. I could share my perspective with others just starting on this journey and help them navigate the early stages better than I did.

It really boils down to expectations. When we have an expectation about how something will be—whether positive or negative—we are basically comparing it to something else. That is a certain recipe for unhappiness, because you'll never be able to re-create that magical moment (for example) you had ten years ago on vacation, so all else pales in comparison. But when you remove the expectation, magic happens every day, multiple times per day. Look at the world through the eyes of your dog and witness this gift that they possess.

Every day, every moment, is their best day ever. They are so filled with joy because they embrace life with every ounce of their being, and are fully present for every moment of it. That is their gift to us, if we are only wise enough to learn from them.

Incontinence

As I watched others in the DM group post their concerns about this disease, one of the biggest concerns was about coping with incontinence. Most people seem to be terribly uncomfortable with the idea of their dog not being able to hold his or her bladder or bowels—and even though we're used to walking our dog and picking up poop in a plastic bag, the idea that it might happen in the house seemed to unnerve most people.

Sassy first became incontinent with her bowels in October 2017. Frequently when I got her up in the morning, she had pooped in her bed

Caring for your DM dog is not for the faint of heart. On any given day you will be exhausted, and feel helpless and overwhelmed by the physical challenges that come with the progression of DM. What your pup could do yesterday may be gone today.

Look for moments of joy because they still exist, they just look different than they did before DM. When you find them, treasure them and remember them. Never let loss rule their life or yours. Find new ways to do things. When your pup's legs fail, use a cart, a wagon or take them for car rides.

They can still smell the air, the earth, and the last place someone peed, so find a way for them to enjoy those simple pleasures. Denby loved lying on the grass watching the world revolve around him. Yes, always a Corgi never just a dog.

Your best friend will lose his ability to walk, run and play but he will never lose his ability to love you. That is one thing DM can never take away.

—Denise & Denby, Pembroke Welsh Corgi

during the night. Fortunately, she was still able to move around enough that she could move away from her poop, so it was very easy to clean up. This was one of those "thresholds" I thought would be really hard to deal with, but it wasn't as bad as my imagination had painted it.

When I saw she had an accident, I picked the poop up in a paper towel, and flushed it down the toilet. It wasn't any harder than picking her poop up outside when we were walking, and I wondered why I ever thought this would be an issue at all.

I quickly learned that expressing (manually stimulating) her bowels before bedtime was the easiest way to manage this level of incontinence. Through trial and error, I figured out what Sassy's "poop schedule" was, and by sticking to that, I was able to mostly control her bowel movements. This reduced the level of accidents dramatically, but she still had them occasionally.

What I initially thought would be terrible to deal with, became easy to do and second nature for me. It certainly wasn't "time" to let Sassy go at this stage. She was bright and alert and enjoying her life still. Her face was full of vitality, and she was still as full of sass as she had always been.

Enjoying a beautiful autumn day, October 2017.

Another New Normal | Miriam Valere

Chapter Eight
A change in attitude

As October 2017 was winding down, I started to see a change in Sassy's attitude about using her cart. There was no denying how much strength her right hind leg had lost. As I would watch her from the behind, her right leg leaned at an angle towards the midline, and her left hind leg was pushing from the outside rather than tracking under her body like it should. The muscle atrophy in her right leg was very noticeable.

It took a lot more encouragement to get her moving in her cart, and she didn't want to walk as far. Walking at this point meant that Sassy moved her front legs, and the weight of her hips and hind legs was being supported by the saddle of the cart. She still moved her left hind leg, but it was losing strength. I attached a leash to the front of her cart, and would pull her slightly to help her start moving, but even doing that, she was resistant to walking. Most days Sassy would only walk a few feet, and then stop.

I started putting Sassy in the wagon more often for walk times with Zeek and Frodo. Sassy loved to get out and enjoy the fresh air, and instead of struggling with getting her to use her cart, the wagon gave us a way to be out together. We took longer walks, and the boys walked as fast as they wanted, so everyone was happy. It was stimulating for Sassy's mind to be outside, even if her body wasn't getting as much exercise.

In hydrotherapy, it was obvious that she was weakening, and her right hind paw was dragging. Tiffany or Lauryn would sit behind Sassy in the tank and manually move her right hind leg. There was a spinal reflex that could be triggered by manually moving her leg, so her weakest leg still received some benefit from making a walking movement—but it was only a matter of time now until she lost all use of that leg.

Along with these changes was the realization that her left hind leg was also noticeably weaker. It was undoubtedly taking much more effort to propel herself forward. Tiffany recommended that I get a no-knuckling sock for her left foot to use during hydrotherapy. This is a device that is worn on the leg, and it has a loop that attached over the middle two toes and pulls upward, helping that foot "flip" into the correct position as the dog takes a step. (Note: For dogs with DM using this type of assistive device longer term, rather than for short-term rehabilitation, it is recommended to get the boot with the ring on the toe, to attach the device to, rather than attach to the toes. See *Resources* for more information.)

The most heartbreaking issue for me is Addison, who is about to turn nine years old, is perfectly healthy in every other aspect and she still has a puppy personality. To see her get so excited when I come home, only to see her hind legs splay like a deer on ice is just so sad. The anguish that comes as the disease progresses is overwhelming; do I let her go once her hind legs are completely paralyzed and she can't go to the bathroom on her own? Do I use wheels and diapers to prolong her life? Am I being selfish by doing so? She's not in pain; she's such a happy girl, yet I see the frustration in her daily struggles. This is the canine version of ALS and it is so heartbreaking for our four-legged kids to suffer this horrible affliction.

—*Jim Dolan*
Addison,
Bernese Mountain Dog

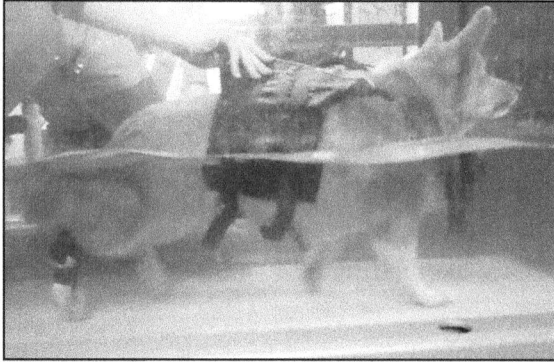

Sassy using the no-knuckling sock during hydrotherapy.

DM is a devastating disease! There is nothing "painless" about it! The look in my Iris's eyes was heartbreaking. She would look at me as if she was saying 'Momma, why can't I walk?' She was totally dependent on me for everything. She was anxiety ridden and afraid to be out of my sight, was unable to sleep in her bed because she could not right herself if she rolled over, and sometimes she was afraid of the dark and would cry all night. A DM afflicted dog requires 24 hour per day care. It was emotionally and physically exhausting but I would do it again without hesitation! Iris was my heart dog.

—Iris's Mom
Pembroke Welsh Corgi

By mid-November, I realized that Sassy was no longer strong enough with her left hind leg to push herself into a seal walk. My heart sank at the implications of that. My girl was almost "down" in the back. That is the expression people in the DM community use to describe paralysis of both hind legs. I wasn't ready for this. Sassy had been going so strong through the first half of October, and even though she couldn't use her right hind leg anymore, I thought we had several more months with use of her left hind leg. It seemed like the timing of her disease progression rapidly increased within just a couple of weeks. Despite my best efforts to stay present, my emotions fluctuated wildly from calm acceptance, to anger, to tears of frustration, and to denial. As Sassy went through the stages of DM, I went through the stages of grief.

I'm tired

Sassy hadn't been able to navigate the three steps outside to the backyard since early summer. At first, I would take her cart outside, pick Sassy up, and put her in her cart. Sassy had never liked being picked up, and would struggle to get out of my arms, which made this process challenging. I tried a new tactic of putting her in her cart in the house, and then lifted her up, wheels and all, to carry her outside. That worked better, but the result was my forearms became badly bruised and sore from picking her up this way. I had intended to build a ramp during the summer so she could roll out on her own, but didn't have the time or energy to do that. My lower back ached from bending down to give her a gentle push to get her moving multiple times per day. My left shoulder had a deep, burning pain in it from the physical strain of lifting her so frequently and carrying her from room to room.

This level of caregiving was becoming physically very difficult for me. All my aches and pains, not to mention the unrelenting fatigue, reminded me every day of how much I was doing with Sassy. Once again, I was very grateful that Sassy was a 30-pound corgi, rather than one of the larger breeds that are prone to DM, like German Shepherds or Boxers. I was in awe of the caregivers who coped with this disease with their 110-pound dog.

Another New Normal | Miriam Valere

I also have fibromyalgia, and everything I do physically takes a toll on my energy levels. To remain functional, I had learned over the years to carefully monitor my activity and stress levels. As my caregiving for Sassy increased, I had to decide what was most important every day. It was becoming challenging to work full-time and handle the multiple interruptions I had each day with Sassy's care, so I reduced my work hours—many days only putting in three or four hours of billable time. While working less hours helped me cope physically, it created additional stress financially. I was barely making enough to cover my basic expenses, and debt was piling up on my credit cards, despite living as frugally as possible. I told myself this was a temporary situation, and I'd have the rest of my life to pay down my debt after Sassy was no longer with me.

I've always been a nurturer to my core, but this was hard work. Taking care of another person, you generally have the ability to communicate with each other, but with a dog, I had to guess at what Sassy's needs were. Some of her cues were really obvious to me, but most of the time I felt like I was playing a guessing game with her. She would stare at me and make a soft noise to get my attention. No matter what I was doing, I had to stay alert to her vocalizations, the movements she made in bed as she tried to turn herself, the rhythm of her breathing—all of those things gave me subtle clues into her needs. I stayed vigilant until I heard her breathing change to the deep, slow breaths she took when she fell asleep—then I could tiptoe out of the room to take a shower, or get dinner started.

Sassy was equally tuned into me, and would be awake and looking around for me when I got back to where she had been sleeping. As much as I wanted to stay in the present moment and not worry about the future, I knew this would only get worse as Sassy lost more and more of her mobility.

Despite the bleak realization of what was looming ahead, there were many bright spots. I made a point to spend time with Sassy and the boys every day in a way that was enjoyable to all of us. Sometimes that was as simple as taking a blanket outside on a sunny day, and sitting on the ground next to Sassy to read while she napped next to me, and the boys stretched out nearby. We went to the

When Corbi was fully able bodied, aside from her deep and abiding love, she taught me to play, lighten up. Now, she teaches me patience, to stop, be present, smell the flowers and trees. Her world is much smaller, and exquisitely rich. The geese flying overhead put a blissful look on her face. She tolerates my photo interruptions, barely. She makes me laugh. I only wish I were as wise as my Corbi is.

—*Marisalena Manchego*
Corbi,
Pembroke Welsh Corgi

Sassy is now almost fully paralyzed in her hind legs.

*The last photo I have of
Sassy in an upright position.*

park frequently, and sometimes stopped by the pet supply store in my neighborhood to get special treats. One day Sassy surprised me and took off running in her cart, barking enthusiastically when she saw Zeek chasing a squirrel. I cried with joy to see her running again. I don't know how she mustered the strength to run that day, but it warmed my heart to see her so excited.

November 2017 ended with Sassy no longer being able to push herself into a sitting position, a fact that didn't fully register in my mind until two months later. This disease was getting very real now. Sassy had been so willing to adjust to using her cart initially, and had taken everything in stride, completely unfazed by all the changes. Now she didn't want to walk at all. I'd take her into the backyard in her cart and attempt to coax her with treats, she'd walk a few steps, and then stop. Her posture took on a wide-legged stance with her front legs.

I emailed photographs and a video of Sassy to Eddie's Wheels to ask their advice. Being the experts on their cart design, they were able to look at photographs or videos and frequently make recommendations for adjustments so the cart fit more comfortably. I hoped they would have a suggestion for adjusting Sassy's cart that would make it easier for her to use.

One of the features of the Eddie's Wheels cart is what is referred to as a *variable axle*. This allows the rear wheels to be moved forward, which helps to counter-balance the dog's weight as they get weaker in front. After they reviewed the photographs I sent and the video of Sassy walking a short distance, they recommended that it was time to move the wheels forward to help offset her weight. They explained that a dog carries most of its weight in the front part of the body, and in healthy dogs, the rear legs and torso help support that weight distribution. But with a DM dog, as the rear legs become paralyzed, and the torso loses core strength and becomes more flaccid from the disease progression, all of that weight is on the front legs. They said the wide-legged stance I was seeing was Sassy bracing herself to support her weight.

I took their advice, and adjusted the wheels forward. It helped for about two weeks, and then Sassy was right back to her braced position. She

Another New Normal | Miriam Valere

showed no motivation to walk more than a few steps in her cart each day. I knew that at some point Sassy would become too weak to walk, but I was unprepared for what looked like her giving up.

Sassy had always been a dog of substantial attitude, even in her younger, healthy years. I recalled numerous times when I had first adopted Sassy, she would lie down halfway through our walk and refuse to budge unless I turned around and headed for home. Sometimes in exasperation, I would let her lie where she was, and walk Zeek to the end of the block, then turn around and head back to where I left her. She would be belly up, kicking her paws in the air, enjoying the grass, or stretched out with a blissed-out look on her face. As soon as she saw me, she'd happily jump to her feet and trot home the minute she realized that was the direction we were headed. She liked to do things her way, and only her way.

Note the way Sassy is holding her front legs so wide apart. This position gave her more stability to she could support her body weight.

She was perhaps the most stubborn dog I had ever encountered. I hoped that what I was seeing was yet another manifestation of her stubbornness, and that I'd find some way to motivate her to continue walking in her cart.

Still smiling, still sassy!

Chapter Nine
January 2018—another year, another new normal

I followed up with Eddie's Wheels, and let them know that moving the rear wheels forward on Sassy's cart only made a short-term improvement. They suggested it was time to make her cart a quad with the addition of front wheels. She would also need a belly band to provide more support for her abdomen. With her muscles weakening as the disease progressed, her torso was becoming flaccid and starting to sag.

The need for adding front wheels to her cart coincided with Tiffany mentioning that she was only filling the underwater treadmill with eight inches of water now, instead of the ten inches we had initially started with. I could see that Sassy was holding her body lower to the ground—it was like she was shrinking in height. The muscle atrophy in her hips and hind legs was becoming more noticeable now, as her muscles slowly wasted away. The reality was settling in with full force—Sassy's condition was declining.

I ordered the front wheels for her cart, and received them a few days later. I left the front wheels in the box for three days; I just couldn't bring myself to add them. It felt like I was admitting defeat and giving in to this horrible disease. At that moment, I hated DM more than I thought possible. It was so unfair that Sassy had to go through this. I knew it wasn't productive to wallow in self-pity about this disease, and it certainly wasn't helping Sassy any, so I forced myself to snap out of my bad mood. This is what life handed Sassy, and I had to deal with it and learn to cope. Sassy was depending on me to take care of her.

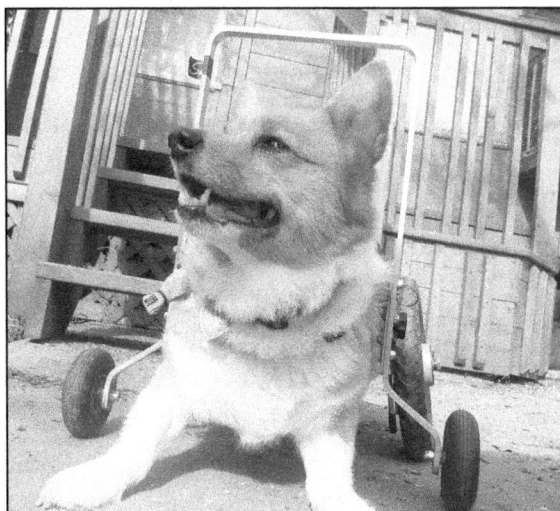

Front wheels added to give Sassy more stability. See how much lower to the ground she is holding her body. Even with the added front wheel support, she was still struggling to support her weight.

> Trying to keep positive has been rough knowing I'm powerless over the progression of this ugly disease. It's extremely saddening to watch my old girl struggle and there's not a thing I can do about it. I smile big for her but cry most nights when she can't see me.
>
> —*Lauren Dill*
> *Minnie, Great Pyrenees*

I added the front wheels on January 20, 2018—almost exactly one year after Sassy started hydrotherapy. The new challenge this presented became readily apparent. While the front wheels provided more stability for her it also made her cart heavier and more awkward to turn. Sassy hated it and didn't want to walk at all now. I didn't know what to do. Based on how she was still walking in hydrotherapy, it looked like she had enough front leg strength that surely, she could still walk. I simply could not figure out how to motivate her.

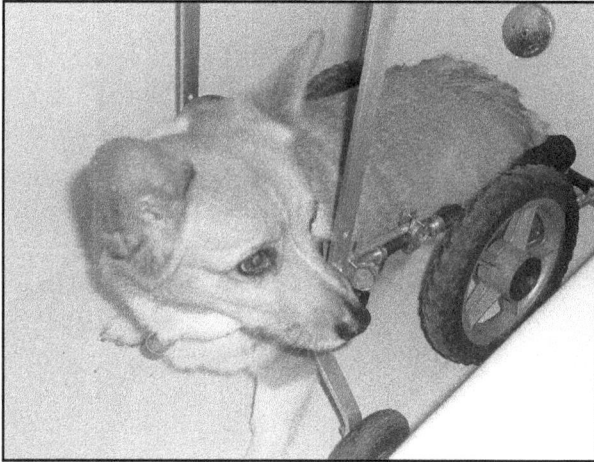

In the bathtub, cart and all, to clean up after urinary incontinence.

Sassy also became urinary incontinent during this same time. I started putting potty pads under her in an effort to minimize the amount of laundry I needed to do as a result of her wetting her bedding. Invariably, she would somehow scoot herself off the potty pad, so I was doing a load of laundry almost daily. I also had to bathe her whenever she had an accident, as I didn't want her to get urine scalds. Even though she didn't seem to mind getting wet during hydrotherapy, she hated getting a bath. She was surprisingly strong as she scrambled to retain her footing in the tub, and tried to get out of my arms. I felt like I was wrestling a greased pig when she struggled like that. After a few days of getting myself soaked in the process of bathing her, I figured out that I could put her in her cart, and then place her and the cart in the bathtub. She was able to stand and not lose her footing in the tub, and it made the process so much easier. I'd position her back end close to the faucet, and filling a container with water, I was able to quickly rinse her hind legs. Then I would lift her out of her cart, wrap her in a towel and dry her off. As much as she hated bath time, Sassy loved the drying off time, along with the belly rubs I'd give her. I'd roll her over on her back, and her floppy, paralyzed back legs would twitch as I massaged her legs. She always had a big grin on her face as she got her belly rubs.

I was concerned that Sassy would be upset that she had lost control of her bladder in the house, but she didn't seem to react to that at all. I was grateful that this latest change didn't seem to bother her. The only discomfort I saw from her was when her bedding was wet and she wanted to move away. I don't know if she could still feel the sensation of "wet" at this point, or if she disliked the smell of urine, and was moving away from the scent.

Once she settled down to sleep, she typically was fairly quiet and didn't move around much. But I could always tell when she had urinated in bed, because she got very fussy, made soft whines, and fidgeted in her bed. Sometimes she even pulled herself completely out of her bed and I would find her on the floor next to her bed.

I felt like I had adapted very quickly to her being bowel incontinent, but this latest change was much harder to cope with, and I now understood

Another New Normal | Miriam Valere

why so many people in the DM group worried about this stage. Between the extra laundry and the baths, there was so much more work involved with this than just picking up poop in a paper towel.

I knew that once I learned how to express her bladder, I would be able to manage her incontinence better by keeping her on a schedule. At first, I really struggled to feel her bladder—this was trickier than I had expected. I looked at diagrams showing the anatomy of a dog, and palpated her abdomen, hoping I could feel that little balloon full of urine. Sometimes she'd start urinating before I had a chance to really palpate her abdomen, and I couldn't figure out what I had pressed on that helped her release her urine. Through trial and error, I found some techniques that worked for a while, such as having her balance on her front legs without her cart, and I would put my forearm under her abdomen just in front of her hind legs to support her back end and hold her upright. That put enough pressure on her bladder to allow her to urinate. After much practice, I was finally able to quickly find her bladder and express her urine. All the fumbling around was worth the effort because it definitely made this stage more manageable to deal with.

I thought this would be an awful stage to be at, and at first it was overwhelming. After about a month of urinary incontinence, I could see this was simply another aspect of caring for Sassy. As long as I stayed consistent with taking her out for a potty break every 3–4 hours during the day, and right before bedtime, this stage was manageable.

Some days are more challenging

One day I had to run an errand after I ended my work day. Sassy was sound asleep in her bed, so I decided to take her out for a potty break when I got back home. I had taken her out about two hours earlier, so I thought I'd be back before she needed to relieve herself again. I was only gone about fifty minutes, and got home to find her

When we adopted our beautiful mixed breed Brodie, we thought his grab bag of genes would keep him safe from the congenital diseases that often plague purebred dogs. But in his ninth year, that rogue GSD gene asserted itself and he developed DM. And so, we started down the heartbreaking journey of loving, caring for, and ultimately releasing our boy. What we have learned is that most vets don't know as much about DM as we owners do. The DM Facebook page was full of incredibly helpful information, such as feeding pumpkin to firm up stools, applying ice cubes to express said stools, where to buy the invaluable Help 'Em Up Harness, and so much more. Brodie himself taught us how to care for him by learning to poop while lying on his side after he was down in the back and never complaining when in his sling or harness. He also gave us the incredible gift of discovering our capacity for patience and compassion, as the disease progressed and his care became more complex. Many hours were spent standing under the constellation Canis Major waiting for him to do his business before bed. Letting him go was the hardest decision we have ever had to make, but whenever we look up in the night sky and see the Dog Star, we think of Brodie and know that we did everything for him that was humanly possible.

—*Bonnie Kopp*
Brodie, Lab/Shepherd/Mix

halfway off her bed, the potty pad and her blanket completely soaked. I was irritated with myself that I hadn't taken her out before I left, and now she was distressed because she was laying in urine-soaked bedding, and I wasn't there to help her. I picked her up so I could get her cleaned up, only to have her start urinating—a lot. Now my jeans and my shoes were soaked, along with the rug I had been standing on. And then she pooped as well.

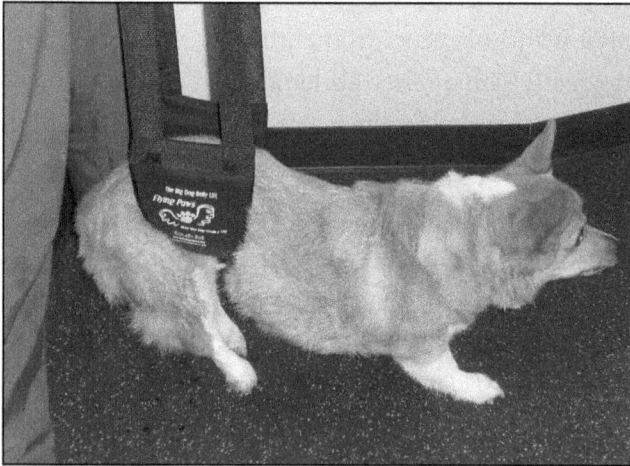

Sassy using a Flying Paws sling during physical therapy.

So, instead of getting dinner ready as I had planned, I had Sassy in the bathtub and gave her a bath. Once I got her clean and rinsed off, I wrapped her in a towel and dried her off. Then I changed my clothes, and got yet another load of laundry in the washing machine.

Some days were like that.

A new lease on life

January 26, 2018 marked Sassy's one year in hydrotherapy. She was able to walk about sixteen minutes each session with a couple of rest breaks.

Pat was filling in for Tiffany that day, and it had been several months since she had last seen Sassy. I mentioned during that session how my body was taking a beating from carrying her from room to room now that Sassy didn't want to walk in her cart anymore. Pat suggested we try walking Sassy with a sling to see how she did. The sling was like a broad belt that fit under Sassy's belly, and had long handles so I could lift her hind end up with her back legs off the ground, and that position supported most of her body weight. In this "wheel barrow" position, she could move her front legs to walk. To my surprise and delight, Sassy took off at a fast walk in the sling. I was stunned to see her moving so well.

I had thought Sassy was almost done walking because her front legs had become too weak, but with the sling supporting most of her weight, Sassy

Another New Normal | Miriam Valere

showed great interest in using her front legs again and moving. I didn't hesitate and purchased the sling. It was life-changing.

After a few days of walking around the backyard using the sling, Sassy made it clear that she wanted to walk more, so I took her out on the sidewalk and she happily walked with her front legs to the end of the street and back. A few days later, Sassy walked in this manner across the street to the park that was near my house and back, and thoroughly enjoyed exploring all the smells in the park. This was the longest she had walked in months! While I supported her back end, she'd stand and bark at dogs she saw walking by. I was so excited to see this change in her. I felt hopeful again. Maybe with the help of the sling, I'd be able to give her the necessary exercise to keep her front legs strong for a while longer.

Sassy taking a walk using her sling.

This was an important lesson for me about not getting fixed in my thinking. I had been so focused on getting her to walk using her cart, that I overlooked a very simple solution that worked beautifully for her.

The sessions with her physical therapists were helpful on many levels. They could see Sassy with different eyes than I did, and were able to make suggestions on how to manage her care better. Being trained both in human physical therapy as well as canine therapy, they invariably gave me helpful pointers on how to ease the strain on my body as well. The emotional support I received each week proved invaluable. Some days when I felt depressed about her condition, they were able to show me things that she was still doing well, or exercises I could do to help keep her stronger. It gave a semblance of control in this journey that now seemed to be mostly about losing control day by day.

Chapter Ten
Unexpected news

At the end of January 2018, Frodo had a very restless night and woke me up twice to go outside, something that he never did. In the morning, I found several places where he had accidents throughout the house—and those were diarrhea with a noticeable amount of blood. I was very alarmed, and knew this could be serious. I called the vet as soon as they opened, and got him in right away. As the vet was sitting on the floor examining Frodo and asking me questions, she said, "He has a mass. We need to look at this."

Before I really had a chance to think about what she was saying, the vet took Frodo in the back to do a quick ultrasound. She came back with serious news. Frodo had a mass on his spleen. It could be a large hematoma, or it could be cancer, but the end result was the same—if his spleen wasn't removed right away, it would be fatal if it ruptured.

I immediately questioned putting a 15-year-old dog through such a major surgery. The vet said that was a valid question, but stressed the urgency of making a decision. She said their best vet for doing a splenectomy had an opening on Friday morning. She suggested that we take chest X-rays, do a complete blood panel, and send Frodo to an ultrasound specialist. She said with better ultrasound equipment than they had at their office, and an internal medicine vet who was highly trained to read ultrasounds, we might be able to determine if Frodo already had signs of cancer throughout his abdomen. If

Frodo getting his ultrasound.

that was the case, surgery wasn't recommended, and he would be essentially on hospice care to keep him comfortable. I was an emotional wreck by this point and not sure I was processing the information very clearly.

I contacted my animal communicator, Valerie, to ask her if Frodo was strong enough to do the surgery. She said his life force felt strong to her, and that he definitely wanted the chance to live longer. But she also shared a message from him: Frodo wanted me to know that he had experienced so much love in the few months that we had been together, that to him, it felt like he had a lifetime of love. He told her that every day we had together was a bonus day to him, and that he was grateful for the love I gave him. My sweet, old gentleman was telling me in his special way that if he didn't survive the surgery, that he had no regrets, and neither should I.

The day of the second ultrasound, Frodo was as relaxed and happy as always. As the specialist moved the ultrasound wand over all of his abdomen, he pointed out what he was seeing. He showed me the mass on the spleen, then he moved on to the liver and made note of a couple areas that might be of concern. He also noticed a small mass on one adrenal gland and explained that it's a very hard area to biopsy, and difficult to remove an adrenal gland.

Based on what he saw, he didn't feel there were any obvious signs of metastatic cancer. Frodo's chest X-rays and blood work came back with no issues, so he was a good candidate for the surgery. Almost before I could catch my breath, everything fell into place for Frodo to have his spleen removed on Friday.

Running on empty

Frodo came through his surgery very well, though he was slow to come out of the anesthesia. I turned the living room into a recovery room, and slept on an air mattress on the floor next to Frodo so I could wake up quickly if he needed anything.

Our "recovery" room sleeping arrangements on the living room floor.

Frodo wasn't supposed to go up and down steps for two weeks, so I was lifting and carrying him outside whenever he needed to go potty, in addition to carrying Sassy outside multiple times per day. I joked about my corgi workout program, but inside I was close to a breaking point.

Caring for both Sassy and Frodo at the same time tested my caregiving skills, and I was running on empty. I was sleeping on the living room floor with Frodo next to me, and Zeek and Sassy sleeping nearby. I hadn't gotten a good night's sleep in several days because any sound one of the dogs made woke me up. When Frodo became uncomfortable or needed to go outside to potty, I was instantly awake. I was close to exhaustion when he finally slept all night long. What a difference a solid night's sleep made for my attitude.

A week later, Sassy started to have diarrhea. The mess was awful. I took her out on her regular schedule, but she was having several accidents a day in her bed. I had to bathe her each time it happened. I used my technique of putting her in the bathtub, cart and all, and ran water over her back end and legs, then massaged the shampoo into her fur, and rinsed. I'd lift her out of her cart, and wrap her in a towel to dry her off. And then a couple hours later, I would have to do it all over again with her next accident. After two days of that, I sat on the floor and cried from exhaustion and frustration.

Normally, I have a very even temperament, and don't get angry often, but I could feel myself becoming very short-tempered. My cats took the brunt of the frustration I was feeling. If one of my cats wanted attention and started to headbutt me, or stretched out in front of my keyboard when I was working, I reacted angrily, and brusquely pushed him away. It pained me to respond like that, but I was so drained from a week of doing double-duty caregiving on top of the previous full year of caregiving, that I didn't have anything left to give.

I had tried to get Sassy's diarrhea under control by fasting her one day, and then giving her boiled chicken and rice the next day. That helped a little, but didn't clear it up, so I took her to the vet, and found out she had an intestinal bacterial infection. She started on antibiotics and a probiotic, and I was so thankful when she didn't have any accidents the next day. The third day after starting those medications, her poop was looking more solid. It's amazing how seeing fairly normal poop can feel like the best gift you've ever received.

Frodo continued to recover, and a week after his surgery, he was acting like his old self again. I started to cautiously let him go down the steps by himself, which gave my body a much-needed break from lifting. There was light at the end of the tunnel.

Wake-up call

Taking care of one dog recovering from surgery, and the added challenge of Sassy having diarrhea was all it took for me to be completely drained. This was a wake-up call to me to start taking better care of myself. I couldn't afford to get sick myself, or I wouldn't be able to care for Sassy. I struggled to restore the fragile balance I needed to cope.

I somehow managed to keep my fibromyalgia from flaring up with all the extra stress from the past two weeks. It felt like I was walking on a tightrope where one false step would cause me to fall; keeping my fibromyalgia in check forced me to prioritize each day by what was most important. I had to take care of myself, I had to care for my animals, and I had to work—those were my daily must-dos. Everything else was non-essential and would have to wait.

One area that I really struggled with was the housework. My house was a mess. It looked like a hoarder lived there. I had stacks of unopened mail sitting on the dining room table. The table was covered with things I needed to put away. I had never been a fanatic about having a spotless house, but it used to at least be tidy, and I could sit at my table to eat a meal.

Lately, I felt embarrassed when friends stopped by, and I was critical towards myself about my lack of initiative in keeping the house clean. It was February 10, and my Christmas tree was still up. I told myself for the last month that it was time to put it away—and there it was, still decorated. The amount of energy needed to get the boxes out of the basement and pack away the ornaments felt daunting to me.

The reality was, I didn't have any more of "me" to give away at the end of the day. I was stretched very thin with taking care of all of my animals (six cats in addition to the dogs), and Sassy's care was increasing every month, whether I wanted to admit it or not. The housework would have to wait.

Changing entrenched habits

It was hard for me to put myself first. For most of my life, I had the tendency to take care of everyone around me before ever considering my needs—or even realizing that I had needs. But I also knew how precarious my energy reserves were right now. If I didn't take care of myself, I might very well get some much-needed downtime, but it would be in the form of illness, and getting sick wasn't an option right now. I had too many animals relying on me. Just like being on an airplane and being told to "Put your oxygen mask on before helping others," I wasn't going to be much good to anyone else if I was sick, or if I had a bad fibromyalgia flare and was unable to function. The pain and fatigue from my fibromyalgia flares had been debilitating in the past, and I had no desire to ever return to that level of dysfunction. I had worked too hard to get my symptoms under control to backslide now.

Once again, I made a silent prayer of thanks that if anyone in the household had to have ALS, it was Sassy and not me. I cannot imagine how challenging my life would be if I were the one with this awful disease.

I knew I wouldn't be able to break a lifetime of habits of putting myself last overnight, so I started with some small changes initially so that my mind would not be so resistant to making change. I approached it the same way I approached getting in better physical condition. If I had a goal of walking two miles a day, I wouldn't attempt to walk that distance the first day I started to exercise. I would break it down into smaller goals at first; walk a quarter mile daily for two weeks, and then increase to a half mile, and continue to increase slowly until I hit my goal. From experience, I learned that was the best way to avoid sore muscles and making myself overly exhausted. If this approach worked for me physically, it would surely work for me emotionally as well.

Initially, I focused on being grateful. I felt gratitude was the best place to start, because feeling grateful has a way of changing the way you see the world and your problems.

As I went to bed each night, and before getting up in the morning, I would breathe deeply and think about what I was grateful for in that moment.

> *I am grateful for the love of my friends and family.*
>
> *I am grateful for electricity.*
>
> *I am grateful that I can work from home.*
>
> *I am grateful that I live near the mountains.*
>
> *I am grateful for hot water.*
>
> *I am grateful for the birds singing in the tree outside.*
>
> *I am grateful for my cat purring on my shoulder.*
>
> *I am grateful that I have so many wonderful animals in my life.*
>
> *I am grateful for the challenges in my life that force me to grow.*
>
> *I am grateful that I can read.*
>
> *I am grateful that I am curious.*
>
> *I am grateful for beautiful music.*

As I sat at my computer to start each work day, I would read an inspirational quote or motivational message before tackling my tasks—anything that put me in a positive frame of mind and uplifted me. I found nature-sounds playlists as well as meditation and reiki music on YouTube, and played those softly in the background. The soothing music helped me to relax while I worked. Every couple of hours, I would take a short break,

You will never regret the DM journey you make with your dog. You will bear witness to your dog's courage, strength and everyday heroism.

You will be humbled by their ability to live in the moment and to find joy in life even when it appears there is no reason for it to still exist.

You will rant and rage against DM many times throughout the journey but you will never, ever regret having made the journey.

—*Denise & Denby,*
Pembroke Welsh Corgi

stretch, and look at some beautiful nature photographs for a few minutes to refresh my mind.

At first, it was an effort to remember to do these things, and my mind would drift into thinking about what's next on my to-do list, or whatever was worrying me the most. But with practice, I found that I could focus more clearly on gratitude, and that each day I had more things I felt grateful for.

My heart started to feel lighter and more joyful. I found pleasure in doing the simplest of tasks, as I became more focused on being present in each moment. Household chores, like doing the laundry or the dishes, no longer felt so much like work. My attitude towards chores shifted from *I have to do this* to *I get to do this.* That subtle change made something that was previously a burden feel more like a gift.

My bond with Sassy deepened, and I started to feel what an honor it was to care for her. There was a sense of joy that was flowing through me more often.

I gave myself permission to have a few moments every day just for me. When the weather was mild, I would stretch out in my hammock for a few minutes during my lunch break, shut my eyes, and relish the warmth of the sunshine on my face. I sat and looked at the sky, and whether it was full of clouds, or breathtakingly blue, I soaked in the beauty. I admired the sunsets in their full glory. At night, I'd pause when taking the dogs out for their bedtime potty break, and look at the stars and the moon shining so brightly in the sky. *Thank you for this beautiful world* was my silent prayer to God.

Still needing a vacation, but unable to afford it with all the extra expenses of caring for Sassy, I started to spend more time looking at vacation photos my friends and family were posting on social media, and lived vicariously through their experiences. I let myself imagine what it felt like to be sitting on that beach in Hawaii, exploring the Canadian Rockies, or eating at that sidewalk cafe in Paris. Instead of feeling resentful that I wasn't able to take a vacation right now, I relished the idea that I could have so many different experiences through the eyes of my friends. Slowly, I started to feel more refreshed. It was a start to some much-needed self-healing.

Chapter Eleven
Eighteen months and counting

I looked at Sassy sleeping in her bed; this wasn't her fault and she didn't deserve this disease any more than any other dog that has it. And she certainly didn't ever deserve me being short tempered or impatient with her. But I am only human, and some days I did feel impatient when she wouldn't urinate, despite my best attempts at expressing her bladder. It was frustrating when I was in a hurry, and I'd try for several minutes with no results, so I'd give up and take Sassy back inside— only to have her urinate thirty minutes later in her bed.

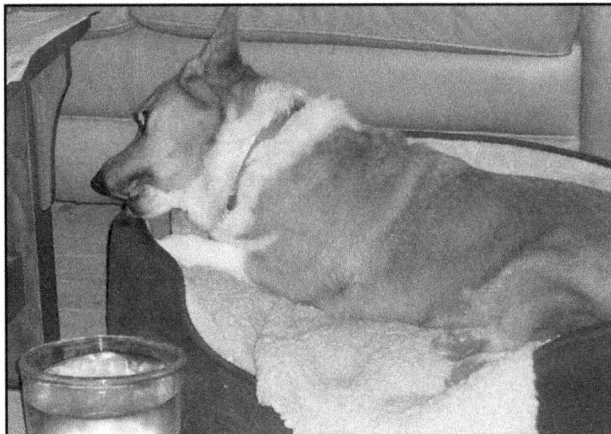

Sassy at eighteen months post-onset of symptoms, relaxing in her bed.

I apologized to her daily for my inability to handle her disease with as much grace as she did. She was the better of the two of us, and I hoped that before she died, that I would be as present and accepting as she was.

At eighteen months into this journey, I wondered—*will I have another eighteen months with her? Or will it be six more months?* Many dogs do not survive this disease past two years. Sometimes that is because the dog reaches a point where their owners can no longer cope with the disease, or because the dog became too anxious and unhappy, and sometimes the dog developed a secondary illness that compromised his quality of life too much.

Sassy didn't have too much anxiety at this point, unless she couldn't see me. As long as I was in the same room with her, she was content. If I went to the bathroom, or into the kitchen, Sassy would start to bark and become upset. I started to pick her up and carry her from room to room if I needed to be in a different part of the house for more than a few minutes.

Of course, the fact she was so dependent on me made it difficult for me to leave her for any length of time. I didn't feel comfortable with other people watching Sassy for me, though occasionally, Tina would come by to sit with Sassy to give me some time to myself. I kept my errand-running and other activities away from home to be under two hours at any one time. I felt anxious to be away from her even for that short of a time, worried that she needed me and I wouldn't be there to help her. I didn't go out to movies or concerts anymore. The only parties I went to were ones happening in my neighborhood, where I could either bring Sassy with me, or run home every hour to check on Sassy. It felt like my world was collapsing in on itself and becoming very small.

Yet at the same time I had been living in this microcosm, I was getting glimpses into this larger world that my dogs live in. The sheer bliss of being outside on a warm day sniffing the wind. The excitement when they saw a squirrel at the bird feeder. The joy of sitting quietly at my feet, getting a scratch behind their ears. Their life was not small or insignificant in any way. They were showing me what joy looks like.

Sassy still had some reflexes in her hind legs and would frequently kick at me when I put her in her cart. But her back legs hung useless for the most part. Her once strong and muscular hind legs were limp and atrophied. I looked back through my photos more often, trying to keep the memory of what it was like when she could still walk, run, or jump up on me. I remembered all the times I said sternly "get down Sassy" when she'd jump on me, and now I would give anything to have her be able to jump up on me one more time. Even though I wanted to stay focused on the present moment with her, the agony of watching the slow, steady decline would creep in. I knew at some point she would lose the use of her front legs, and then it was only a matter of time before she started to go into organ or respiratory failure. Of all the thresholds I had mentally set up until this point, the one I knew was non-negotiable was having Sassy go into end-stage organ or respiratory failure. I knew I would not let her suffer, and it would be time to say goodbye before she reached that stage. I didn't want to think about letting Sassy go.

Even though Sassy and Zeek had been part of my family for two and a half years now, Tina was still very attached to Sassy, and visited her when she could. Between visits, I gave Tina updates on how Sassy was doing. I knew that ultimately the decision to euthanize Sassy would fall on my shoulders, but I felt it was important to include Tina in those discussions so we were in agreement. I didn't want any objections to surface that would put Sassy into a crisis at the end. I made sure that we shared how we each felt about euthanizing Sassy, and discussed quality of life measurements, along with what end-stage symptoms looked like. As hard as those conversations were for both of us, it had to be discussed.

Like so many others going through this, I prayed that Sassy would die in her sleep so I wouldn't have to make the decision for her. I felt heartsick at the idea that I might lose her. My emotions were all over the place; some days I had calm acceptance of the situation, and other days, I was full of grief, or anger that we had to deal with this awful disease. Lately, the tears spilled over easily and frequently, and I was constantly reaching for something to wipe my eyes on.

Sassy's still alert and loving being outside. This is as far as she can push herself upright now.

It is never easy to euthanize a beloved animal companion, but when they are in pain, very ill, or suffering in some way, at least your rational mind knows it is the right thing to do. Many people use loss of appetite as a threshold of when to euthanize an animal. But with the cruelness of DM, your dog can remain alert, bright-eyed, and interested in eating, right up until the last breath. They aren't sick in the usual sense of the word, so things like appetite aren't impacted, unless a secondary illness is present. They still want to interact with you, just like always. But they are paralyzed, and they depend on you for almost everything.

Now that Sassy was losing so much strength in her front legs, I had to remember to change her position every couple of hours so she didn't develop pressure sores. I hadn't figured out how to contend with this at night yet, as my sleep was critical to keeping my fibromyalgia symptoms under control. For now, I was letting her sleep all night and hoped that she was shifting her weight in the night enough on her own to avoid that problem.

I wasn't sure how I was going to handle this disease advancing.

Zoey's DM experience … it was a roller coaster of emotions from highs to absolute lows and all the while my head was filled with thoughts on how I will let her go when the time comes. We laughed so much when she ran like Forrest Gump in her wheels but that thought never went away … RIP my beautiful girl—she was my absolute world.

—*Julie Georgiou*
Zoey Lou,
German Shepherd

Chapter Twelve
Mid-February 2018—a reprieve

Sassy's diarrhea had finally cleared up after a round of antibiotics. Frodo was at his two-week post-op date and had his staples removed. He was able to start going back to his regular activities. I was starting to feel civilized again and not stretched so thin. My efforts at taking care of myself were starting to have a positive effect, and I felt calmer and more grounded each day.

I never expected to be this bound to the care of a dog. Even when Lexx, my first corgi, was dying of lung cancer, he didn't need my help, though sometimes I carried him if he got tired on a walk. But that was not a daily occurrence, let alone multiple times per day occurrence.

I looked at videos of Sassy from late March-April 2017 when I was first working with getting her used to using her wheeled cart. As the summer had progressed, she still moved all four legs, and she walked right up to the steps to the house, and one at a time, put her front paws on the first step, and waited for me to lift the back end of her cart, then walked into the house. As she became weaker in the fall, I started to carry her more. That was one of those things that I didn't consciously think about doing. It was yet another example of adapting to her needs as they occurred. It was strange to look back over the many months of this journey and realize just how often I had modified how I was doing something with her, although in that moment I wasn't conscious at all that I was doing anything differently.

People kept telling me how amazing I was with my care of Sassy. I was not amazing. I was simply responding each day to what she needed, and attempting to keep the quality of her life high. If she had been depressed, in pain, or had some medical condition like cancer, or uncontrollable seizures, it would be understandable to let her go. But she was

I was always reassuring Maggie by saying "Don't worry, I've got you." I had no idea what I was doing with DM, and like all of us who are dealing with it had no direction or knowledge of what our journey would bring. Maggie was always our crazy curly haired girl up to the end. When she lost the use of her back legs it was the lowest point of our journey. I knew she was as scared as we were. But I knew how important it was to let her know "I've got you." My heart was breaking putting on the harness and knowing it would be on indefinitely. It was winter and we would walk each morning on the snow. Me holding her back end up more and more with each walk. Her paw prints and my footprints, the DM so visible in the snow. Those perfect front paw prints and dragging back ones. Then we let her go and slowly each day as I retraced our short morning walk with tears in my eyes and a heavy heart, her dragging prints disappeared and only mine remained. I think of our 12.5-year journey with her and feel blessed. Silently and patiently she became my best friend. She took care of us and always knew when we needed a lick and a cuddle. We have since been blessed with another Kerry puppy. I know Maggie sent her to us—after all she worked so hard teaching us how to love a dog; she would not want her efforts to be in vain. I know she is with me leaping off the porch and wagging her tail. I also know that she is saying to me, "Don't worry, I've got you."

—Maggie's Mom
Kerry Blue Terrier

alert. She was aware. She was interactive. She was happy. This was not a dog who was ready to die yet. We carried on each day.

I knew each day we had together put us one day closer to that inevitable end of the journey. And I knew it would break my heart.

And given the chance, I would do this all over again for Sassy.

The tracks of a paralyzed dog in wheels in the snow.

Photo credit:
John Cunningham

Another New Normal | Miriam Valere

Chapter Thirteen
Silver linings

Using the sling with Sassy had literally changed my life. She was rarely urinary incontinent inside now. It seemed like she was able to empty her bladder more fully from the pressure of the sling on her abdomen. That was an unexpected silver lining, and I felt so grateful for this small return to normalcy with her. It made a huge difference to have her remain dry overnight. We still had poop accidents occasionally—but that was never a problem. It was such a relief to not need to bathe her several times per day.

An even bigger gift was Sassy really wanted to walk while I supported her weight with the sling. By lifting up her back end and taking most of the weight off of her front legs, Sassy was able to move her front legs and take short steps. It reminded me of playing "wheelbarrow" as a child, where someone would hold your legs up and you would "walk" with your hands.

Her attitude became so much more alert and vibrant. She relished stopping to sniff at the trunks of the trees, reading the "dog newspaper" to see what dog had walked by recently. She even tackled wading in the snow while I supported most of her weight. It surprised me that she had enough strength to use her front legs in the snow, but she wanted to do it and she showed me she could.

We had missed three weeks of hydrotherapy between Frodo's surgery and Sassy's bout of diarrhea, and I was concerned that we had lost

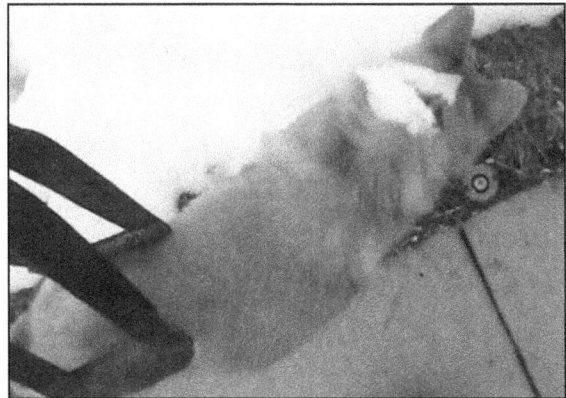

Sassy is still enjoying walking with the sling.

some critical ground. However, all the walking in the sling apparently compensated for the lack of hydrotherapy, because our first day back for physical therapy, Tiffany said she was as strong as she had been before.

Sassy was able to move her front legs very fast in her sling, and sometimes she surprised me and would start to trot. I was delighted by how much she was enjoying this. It made me so happy that she was able to enjoy going out for walks again, even if her mode of walking now only involved her front legs. I found myself feeling light-hearted and full of joy. My heart was full of love and gratitude to see her walking again after I thought she had given up.

Sassy was very alert and interested in what was going on around her. Sometimes I would hear her give a little growl and looked down to see her focused intently on a dog across the street. That was such a huge gift to me, after feeling discouraged for a couple of months due to her lack of interest in using her cart. I regretted that I had been so limited in my thinking during the late fall. I had been so focused on the idea that the only way she could walk was using her cart, that I missed an opportunity for her to be mobile in a simpler way.

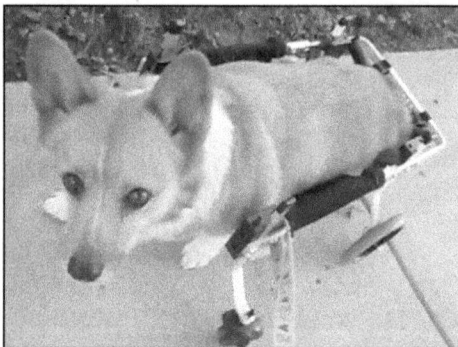

New wheels! Sassy likes her K9 Cart!

New wheels—March 2018

Based on her eagerness to walk in the sling, I took a chance and ordered a different quad cart from K9 Carts West (see *Resources*) in March. This cart had a different type of front wheel, and a much wider belly support that gave her extra abdominal support.

This cart worked really well for her. Sassy exceeded my expectations and was able to easily walk using her front legs in her new cart, her hind legs suspended by straps at the back of the cart. I attached a leash to the front of her cart so I could pull to get her started moving, but she was able to move her front legs on her own power for the most part. During our next hydrotherapy session, Tiffany said that Sassy was stronger in her front legs now than she had been a couple of months ago. I felt hopeful that we had bought ourselves some time, and with spring approaching, I was looking forward to taking Sassy for more walks in her cart again.

I was so excited for this unexpected change—it felt like such a gift. Sassy was happy that she could walk around, sniff, and explore on her own again.

Joyrides and outings

Being with my animals has helped me notice the moments of my life better. But with Sassy, the lessons of living this way were being reinforced moment by moment. On the days when I focused on what was next on my to-do list, I felt impatient and irritated if Sassy took a long time to go potty, or if she were fussy about something. And then I instantly felt chagrined for thinking my priorities were even remotely important in the scheme of things.

In those moments, I would take a deep breath, look up at the sky, notice the brilliant blue, and sigh. I'd say a silent prayer of *Thank you, Sassy, for helping me become a better person.* I would bend down to pat her head, give her a kiss, and tell her how much I loved her.

On the days when I could let myself just be—I noticed the birds at the feeder and singing in the trees around me. I felt the sun on my face, and could let my muscles relax under the warmth of the lengthening days.

Being caught up in the moment, life was full of so many magical and beautiful experiences. Just staying present with Sassy, sitting near her as she held her nose up in the air to

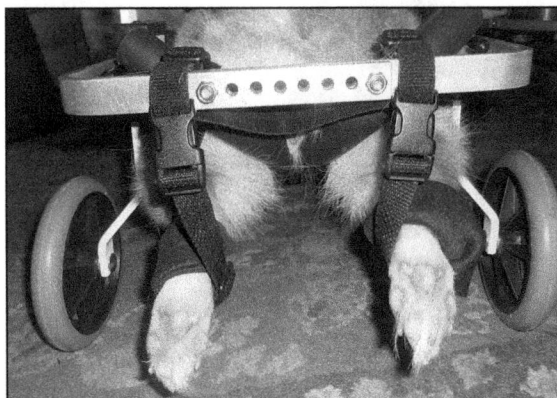

This is how her hind legs are supported in the wheeled cart so they don't drag on the ground.

sniff the wind, or as she barked at a squirrel, was such a blessing. I tried to see life through her eyes, through her senses, and I saw how much she loved to be outside. That was a complete experience for her—she needed nothing more in that moment to be happy.

My thoughts frequently raced ahead to what I needed to do next, rather than just living in the present moment, and that was a source of stress for me. The more I could just "be" in the moment, the more joy I felt. Becoming aware of how often I wasn't present in the moment was the first step to becoming more centered.

On sunny, mild days, I put Sassy in her wagon, and pulled her around the park or the neighborhood while walking Zeek and Frodo. If it was a nice day and the ground was dry, I would let her walk in her cart until she became tired, and then help her roll on the grass. An expression of sheer bliss would be on her face as she stretched out in the sunshine, belly up, her floppy DM legs spread apart, with all the good earthy smells surrounding her. It was restorative for my spirit to sit on the ground

Sassy enjoying a trip to the pet supply store.

next to her and just be in the moment with her. I may not have traveled to any exotic destinations during this time, but I took a journey within my heart and discovered how to be at peace with caring for Sassy. Finally, this path we were on together felt like a special honor to me, and I cherished all the everyday, normal moments we had together.

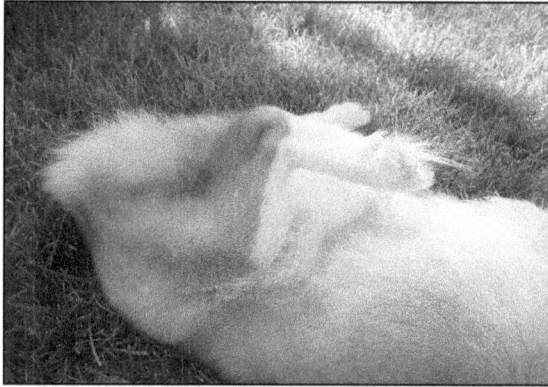

Those darn DM legs. Muscle atrophy in Sassy's hind legs is very prominent now.

We took rides in the car, too. There is nothing quite like a joy ride for a dog. Sassy used to hate riding in the car, and would have to be in her crate, otherwise she would be uncontrollable—I still have ripped fabric in my car from her attacking the dashboard. She started to lose her hearing a couple of years ago, and since that happened, she now enjoyed car rides. Every Saturday I loaded up the car with the three dogs and Sassy's gear, and we went to her hydrotherapy session. If the day was warm, after her session we'd stop at a park on our way home, and relax together in the grass. I took her to our favorite pet supply store so she could explore all the exciting and wonderful smells in the store. We went for many drives up the canyon, the window rolled down so she could smell the evergreens and the fresh mountain air. This was a happy time for both of us.

Having had dogs and German Shepherds all my life, I had never heard of this disease. It came as a shock when Barney was diagnosed. It is a journey that I wish we weren't going through. It is a heartbreaking disease. The deterioration process is soul-destroying for us humans to witness and go through with our fur babies. The only upside is that the dogs feel no pain. He still has a good quality of life. Loves his food, loves his walks and adores his daddy. Every day is a learning curve. And every day is a blessing that we still have him. It is hard work—I won't lie—but we see him as disabled and nothing more. It is hard, he is totally incontinent but we just change his towel under him when required and his dad bathes him morning and night. At first, we could see he didn't understand what was happening to him but we feel now he has accepted his disability and just gets on with it. We treat him as though nothing has changed—he is still top dog and when people come into the house, they go see him so he knows who is here. We believe if you don't make a fuss and treat him normally then he will hopefully carry on for as long as possible. We just want him to be happy.

—*Clare Rosato and Gary Long*
Barney,
German Shepherd

Warmer spring weather was starting, so we spent more time out in the back yard with Sassy on a blanket. I looked forward to working in the soil, planting flowers, gardening, and having my dogs at my side. I loved watching Sassy lift her nose into the air and make a snuffling noise as she found some delightful scent floating by. With her hearing mostly gone, Sassy didn't hear the bird sounds anymore, but she took her cue from Zeek and barked enthusiastically when he started to bark. I used to try to hush her when she'd start barking, and now I treasured hearing her seal bark.

Run, just run

One of the people I had met through the DM groups on Facebook had a passion for spreading awareness about DM through running in 5k races.

Taylor always ran in honor of a dog with DM, and asked me if she could run in Sassy's honor. I was touched by her gesture, and readily agreed. She asked me to write a short story about Sassy and her DM journey that she could post to her Facebook page dedicated to her runs, along with some photos of Sassy.

On race day, Taylor posted photos and videos of all the activities. I didn't expect to feel emotional about this, but when I watched the videos Taylor posted at the beginning of the race, holding Sassy's photo up high as she crossed the starting line, yelling "Run, Sassy, run!" it brought tears to my eyes. I was so touched as she posted her video of nearing the finish line, saying encouraging words like, "Come on, sweet girl, you can do it!" as if Sassy were right there running with her. By the time Taylor crossed the finish line, holding Sassy's photo high in the air, my tears flowed freely.

Taylor ended all of her runs by saying, "We're going to beat this disease. One person. One dog. One breeder. At a time. We can beat this. Because no dog should have to roll. We're going to beat this horrid disease."

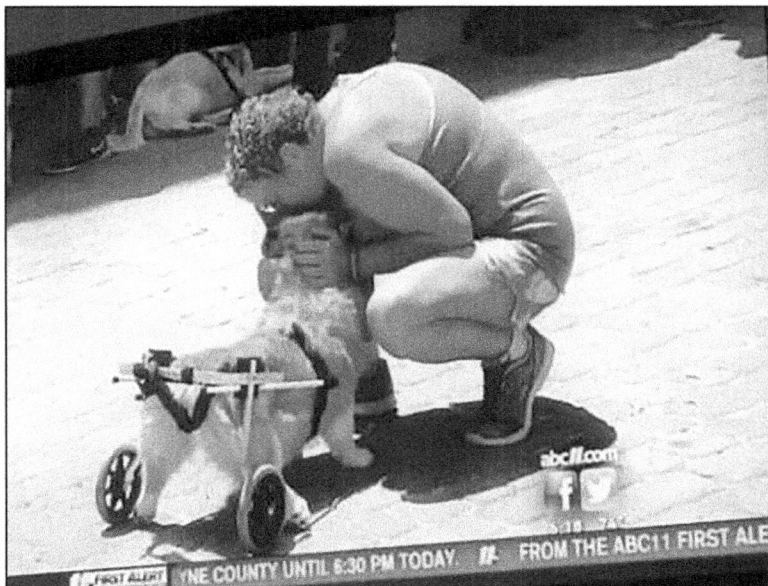

Above, A tender moment of Taylor with Cabo, one of the DM dogs she ran for, captured by a local news station. Taylor puts her heart and soul into her runs, and loves these DM dogs as if they were her own.

Left, "Sassy" crossing the finish line with Taylor.

Taylor runs for those who can't anymore—and since her run for Sassy, I watch all of her videos of the other DM dogs she runs for.

She puts her heart, soul, sweat, and tears into this act of love for DM dogs and their caregivers. To date, she has run more than 30 races with each race honoring a DM dog. I am grateful that she is spreading aware-ness about this awful disease, one run at a time.[4]

4. Connect with Taylor at *Run just run:* https://www.facebook.com/dmawareness/

Chapter Fourteen
April devastation

My day had started like any other. I walked the boys, took Sassy outside, and then fed all the animals. The day seemed normal in every way possible. I had just sat down at my computer to start my work day when Frodo collapsed as he was walking over to his favorite sleeping spot. He slumped against the wall, and then slowly slid onto the floor in a stretched-out position. I rushed to his side and checked his gum color. His gums were pale, and he was panting heavily, his heart pounding. I called his name and he wasn't responsive. I felt like I couldn't breathe, but knew what had to be done. In tears, I called the vet, telling them that I was bringing Frodo in.

After a quick exam, the vet determined that Frodo had massive internal bleeding, and it was time to say goodbye. At 9:15 AM, my sweet boy became an angel.

I was shattered. I had hoped to have him longer; six months wasn't long enough with this sweet, unassuming, and always grateful old gentleman. I wanted to love him more, to take him for more joy rides, to buy him an ice cream cone, to give him a hamburger. It was going to be so difficult not sharing my life with him. You don't realize how hard you can fall in love in a few months, until you have to unexpectedly let them go. I loved him like I loved my first corgi, Lexx, who also had left me six months after I adopted him. It didn't feel fair at all that both of my senior rescue dogs had been taken from me far too soon.

In the days that followed, it was apparent that Zeek was grieving the loss of his walking companion, and he refused to take walks with just me. Zeek made it clear that he preferred walking with Sassy at her slow pace over walking with me alone. Through my tears and heartache, we had to adjust to yet another new normal.

May 2018

I had been noticing a significant difference in how Sassy walked during her hydrotherapy sessions for the past couple of weeks. She was taking shorter steps in the water. She wasn't walking as strongly using her wheels either, so I attached a leash to the front of her cart so I could pull her to help her move.

Zeek was still despondent without Frodo, and I saw him making attempts to befriend Sassy. He would wait until she was asleep, and then he'd lie

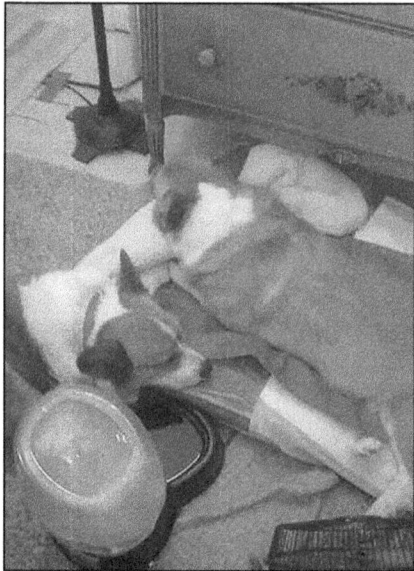

Zeek comforts himself by waiting until Sassy is asleep to be near her.

down right behind her, resting his head on the back of her bed. Even though I expected that we would have several more months with Sassy, I knew that if something happened to her, that Zeek would be beside himself with grief. It was both touching and painful to watch him try so hard to be close to Sassy, especially since Sassy still wanted nothing to do with Zeek.

My heart was not ready to think about adding another rescue to the family, but I was very concerned about Zeek's sadness. He needed a new companion dog. Frodo had been a wonderful addition to our family in so many ways, and the most unexpected way was that he and Zeek formed a strong pack and loved to be together. I think it was the first time that Zeek felt completely safe in the presence of another dog. Now Zeek was missing out on that experience of being part of a pack.

I started to look on the local rescue groups for another corgi, and I told Zeek repeatedly, "Hang in there with me—I'm going to find you a new buddy."

Keeping cool

With the warmer weather, I had to keep a fan pointing at Sassy most of the time, and I had cooling pads that I put under her as well. DM dogs

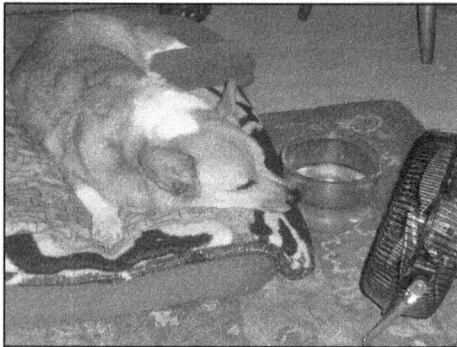

Sassy asleep on her cooling pad, water dish where she can reach it, and fan blowing on her.

are unable to regulate their body temperature, and they easily overheat. I watched Sassy sleeping. Her hind legs twitched; the nerves were misfiring because of the DM. It had a different look to it than when dogs ran in their sleep. It was strange to see her hind legs moving so much when this happened, since she didn't have any movement in them when she was awake.

I took her outside to lay in the grass as often as possible. She enjoyed being out in the yard as I tidied up the garden and planted new flowers. It was therapeutic for me to get my hands in the dirt and make the garden pretty. I created a memory garden for Frodo, and took solace in it every day. I missed my gentle, old man very much.

Mid-May—front leg support

Sassy's decline had become more evident. She wasn't standing as tall in her

Another New Normal | Miriam Valere

cart as she had previously, and it was getting difficult for her to support all of her weight on her front legs, even with the front wheel support. Her cart came with a leg ring support system that was attached between the front wheels, very similar to the rear leg "saddle" that supported her hips and hind legs. After I added the front leg ring support, the leg rings did help to support her chest weight, but they also hindered her range of motion. She started to take even shorter steps, and I knew that would quickly impact her overall front leg

Front leg rings added to her quad cart.

strength. But I didn't have a choice at this point. Without the front leg ring support, it was too hard for her to support her body weight.

Sassy walking with front leg support. Note her head position. It's now getting more difficult for her to hold her head up when walking. Leash is attached to the cart so I can pull her to help her get moving.

Chapter Fifteen
A buddy for Zeek

In early June 2018, I became aware of a little male corgi named Buddy in rescue in Oklahoma. I was absolutely smitten by his sweet face, and it felt like he was "the one." I had some apprehension about adopting a new rescue without a chance to see how Zeek would react to him, but I decided to trust my intuition, and put in an application with Celtic Corgi Rescue on June 7. On June 11, I got the news that they had chosen me to adopt Buddy. *Yes!* A buddy for Zeek, just like I had promised him.

The logistics of getting a dog located in Oklahoma to me in Utah needed to be sorted out. Fortunately, I had a lot of friends in the corgi community on Facebook, so I reached out to a friend in Colorado, and asked her advice. She put me in contact with Karlene Perry, the head of the Wyoming Dachshund and Corgi Rescue (WDCR), and all the pieces began to fall into place. The WDCR frequently used the services of a kind-hearted man who provided transports for rescues, and within a few days, Karlene had the entire transport worked out. Kevin would drive from Wyoming to Oklahoma in one day, spend the night, and pick Buddy up early the next morning from the rescue group. He would then drive to the Denver area and hand Buddy off to my friends there, who would keep Buddy overnight. The next morning, they would drive to Grand Junction, Colorado with Buddy and I would meet them there.

Zeek and Sassy ignoring Buddy (in back).

It was going to be a whirlwind, but all the details fell into place quickly. A local Salt Lake City friend, Madison, offered to make the almost ten-hour round-trip drive with me, so early on June 28, we loaded Zeek and Sassy into Madison's car, and headed to Grand Junction.

It was a very hot day, and we made it to the meeting place around lunch time. I had hoped to spend some time with Josie and Michele before we all headed back to our respective homes—but we were all concerned with the heat, and how hard it was on the dogs, especially Sassy. Buddy was timid, but friendly, and as soon as I picked him up and held him close, I was in love with him. We stopped and bought a bag of ice before heading home, and I packed ice bags around Sassy to keep her comfortable.

Buddy had been kept in an outdoor dog run his entire life, with no vet care at all, so everything about being a well-loved house dog was new to him. Buddy had a chronic dry eye condition, was heartworm positive, and was missing his hind paws. He was a "special needs" adoption. I thought that he would have issues walking on the stumps of his hind legs, but on soft surfaces, like grass, he had no problem at all. The heartworm was a bigger concern, and impacted his stamina, but he seemed happy and full of life despite these challenges.

Buddy settled in quickly and Zeek got his smile back having a new friend.

Zeek was reserved with our new family member initially and mostly ignored Buddy. That was exactly the reaction I had hoped for—ignoring Buddy was much better than acting aggressively. Sassy also ignored Buddy, unless he came too close to where she was resting, and then she'd snap her jaws at him and bark. Buddy was very docile, like Frodo, so when she did that, he scampered away and came to me for comfort and security. He quickly learned not to get in Sassy's space.

Buddy was happy to be inside a house with good food each day, and he settled in quickly.

For me, adding Buddy to the family gave me something else to focus on besides the fact that Sassy's front leg strength was declining faster than I had expected. I enjoyed watching Buddy's personality unfold as he discovered the joys of treats, toys, belly rubs, and sleeping on a soft bed. His playful personality was a bright spot in my life, and a welcome respite from the demands of taking care of Sassy.

Chapter Sixteen
The end of hydrotherapy—July 2018

Sassy had been struggling since late May in hydrotherapy. Each week it was more noticeable. She was having trouble holding her head above water. Tiffany had added a flotation belt under Sassy's torso to see if that would help her, but it didn't have much effect. I bought an inflatable neck support, thinking that might help Sassy hold her head up, but even with that, it was obvious that this therapy was becoming too hard for her.

Using extra flotation support during hydrotherapy

Each week, Tiffany and I had discussed the changes we were seeing, and tried to brainstorm a solution so we could overcome this hurdle. After eighteen months of hydrotherapy, I was reluctant to admit we were finished with this phase. While my logical brain knew that Sassy's condition was degenerative and there was no hope for recovery, I still equated physical therapy with doing something proactive in Sassy's care to slow the progression of the disease. I knew that ending physical therapy would be signaling the beginning of the end.

On July 21, Tiffany put Sassy in the hydrotherapy tank, and started the treadmill. After a few minutes of watching Sassy struggle, her eyes looking panicked, the decision was clear. It was time to stop her hydrotherapy. Tiffany was in agreement with me. We quickly ended the session, and Tiffany spent the remaining time giving Sassy a massage.

Dr. Tiffany Quilter giving Sassy a massage.

I felt awful making that decision. It was much harder than I had expected—our Saturdays had included hydrotherapy for a year and a half, and it had become an important part of our weekly routine. I felt such a close bond with the people at the clinic, and the idea of not seeing them every week felt like an important part of my support network was being cut off.

After I had the dogs loaded back into the car, I sat for a few minutes, with tears running down my face. Along with the sense of loss from ending this important part of our journey was the realization that whether I was ready or not, Sassy's condition was deteriorating.

Vet check and respiration rates

With the end of Sassy's time in hydrotherapy, I felt it was time to take her to the vet to get another set of eyes on her overall health and discuss her quality of life. My biggest worry was respiratory failure, and I wanted to talk to her vet about this, and to get a baseline on Sassy's breathing so we had something to compare it to down the road.

Sassy's vet listened to her lungs, and felt she was breathing without any problems at the moment. The vet recommended that I monitor her breathing at home, and keep a chart of what her resting respiration rate was. By doing that, I'd have my baseline of what was normal for Sassy. An increase in her resting respiration rate of ten or more breaths a minute might indicate she was heading into distress, and it would be time to evaluate her again if I saw that happening. This information gave me a sense of control that I wouldn't be blindsided by a sudden crisis.

I also discussed having a necropsy performed when Sassy died, and donating tissue samples to the University of Missouri, where there was ongoing research and clinical trials for degenerative myelopathy. A necropsy is the term used for an autopsy for an animal. Since we lived too far away to participate in the DM clinical trials being done at the University of Missouri, I felt if Sassy's tissues could contribute to the research, then it would make our journey with this disease worthwhile. With that in mind, two weeks before Sassy's vet visit, I had emailed Dr. Joan Coates, Professor of Neurology and Neurosurgery at the University of Missouri Veterinary Health Center for the list of what tissue samples they were currently requesting for their research. Dr. Coates is one of the researchers who discovered the SOD1 mutation which allowed the DNA test for DM to be developed.[5] She continues to be one of the leading researchers of degenerative myelopathy, and heads up the clinical trials at the University of Missouri. I took the list that Dr. Coates sent me, and Sassy's vet reviewed the list, and indicated that they should be able to do all that was requested.

I felt relieved from that appointment, and was grateful that my vet had spoken so candidly about what to watch for as Sassy's condition progressed. I started to make a habit of tracking Sassy's breathing rate when she was sleeping, and those steady numbers gave me some peace of mind.

5. Awano, T., Johnson, G. S., Wade, C.M., Katz, M.L., Johnson, G. C., Taylor, J. F., Perloski, M., Biagi, T., Baranowska, I., Long, S., March, P. A., Olby, N. J., Shelton, G. D., Khan, S., O'Brien, D. P., Lindblad-Toh, K., & Coates, J. R. (2009). "Genome-wide association analysis reveals a SOD1 mutation in canine degenerative myelopathy that resembles amyotrophic lateral sclerosis." Proceedings of the National Academy of Sciences. 106, 2794-9. 10.1073/pnas.0812297106. Accessed May 5, 2019 through www.pnas.org/content/106/8/2794. abstract

Quality of life scale

The DM group members frequently grappled with the topic of "when is it time" to say goodbye. Group rules mandated that no one ever tell someone they needed to let their dog go unless asked that question directly, as that is a very personal decision. When is the "right time" varies wildly from person to person.

When people posted those questions, some group members would gently direct that person to Scout's House Quality of Life scale (see *Resources*) and suggest they review it to help gain some clarity.

No one wants to think about "the end"—that day you have to make the dreaded decision to euthanize your beloved companion. It is a painful, emotional decision to make, and most people always wonder if they are doing it too soon—or not soon enough. Using a quality of life scale helps you look at your animal's health objectively—and make a decision based on facts, not just emotions. That doesn't make it less painful.

It seems like most people are afraid that they will make the wrong decision, but in my years of caring for animals, I have always felt that if you're asking yourself, *Is it time?* then there is something going on with your animal's condition that is telling you it's time to say goodbye. We hold on tightly, because it's so painful to lose the unconditional love of our beloved animal companions. We don't want to jump the gun and do it too soon—nor do we want to wait too long, and have our animal suffer. There is a saying that is frequently mentioned in the groups: *Don't let your dog's last day be their worst day.* Too often, we hesitate to make that dreaded call, until our dog is in crisis.

When you have a DM dog, there is no absolute "right day" to say goodbye. When the disease has progressed to the point that your dog is no longer enjoying daily activities with you, or is having respiratory difficulties, then it's time to set them free. But if you work outside the home, are caring for young children, elderly parents, or other family members with special needs, or have your own health issues to contend with, then you may find that you aren't able to adequately manage the care of your dog. If that is your situation, you may need to let him go at a much earlier stage—and that is OK. Having a bad back, a recent joint replacement or other surgery, makes caring for a DM dog very difficult. If you struggle with depression or anxiety, it may be overwhelming for you to cope with the care of your dog. Sometimes it's your living environment that presents the challenge—your

We all know it was a lot of work having a half-paralyzed dog; at times it was frustrating, emotional, and as the disease progressed, messy. But taking such intensive care of him, it was a big part of our day. I don't know if anybody who doesn't have a DM dog totally understands. It's like plugging the holes in a failing dam with your fingers but knowing darn well that you can't ultimately stop it from bursting open, all you can hope is to buy time. It wasn't just "he's getting old" ... DM took him from me while the rest of him was fine. He had no idea. We showered him with love and care to give him a damn good quality of life despite the downhill spiral of mobility. Suddenly, that's gone. Silence and stillness and empty space, where just this morning was our daily hustle and bustle. It will take time to get our bearings straight.

—*Lisa Slepetski*
Logan,
German Shepherd

home has a lot of stairs, which means you'll be lifting your dog and navigating stairs at the same time. You have to be honest with yourself about what you can do, and what your limits are. All of these aspects need to be factored in when you have a disabled dog.

Caring for a DM dog is like running a marathon. You start off strong and optimistic about what you need to do, and at some point, you hit that place where you feel you can't take another step forward. Whether you finish that race depends on how much sheer determination and willpower you can pull from your inner reserves. It can take every ounce of your energy to cope with the advanced stages of DM.

Give yourself permission to be at peace about this hard decision. Caring for a DM dog is very labor intensive, and it takes a toll on the caregivers. Be kind to yourself. If you are having trouble coping, if the daily battle is too hard for you emotionally or physically, then be at peace and give your dog a great last week of their life. Your dog won't be upset with you when you set them free. Your dog lives in the moment, and as long as they are with their favorite person, they are happy.

Don't compare your journey with anyone else's. If one person cares for their dog until end stage, and you can only cope until your dog is down in the back, that does not make you less of a person or a bad caregiver compared to someone else. That makes you human, and honest with yourself about what you can do.

This isn't a contest to see who is most devoted to their dog, who has the most stamina, or who is the best caregiver. This is about loving and being with your dog until you are ready to say goodbye. The only thing your dog cares about is that you are there each day with love in your heart. Six good months together can be a lifetime of joy to a dog, so as you confront your dog's growing disability, make memories together. Take lots of photos, go out for a hamburger and an ice cream cone. Take joy rides. **Don't let your fear of tomorrow rob you of the joy of today with your sweet companion.**

Chapter Seventeen
Growing dependency—two years … and counting

At the end of August 2018, our two-year mark from onset of symptoms, I noticed that Sassy was starting to drag her right front paw when she was walking in her cart. The middle two toenails were worn down and I could hear the nails scraping as she walked. It felt like déjà vu—the exact same sound that happened with her right hind foot two years ago. She was taking such short little steps and struggled so much that I knew there wasn't much benefit to be gained from keeping her in her cart at this point.

Tiffany came to visit Sassy and gave her a massage. She explained to me that the muscles on the back side of her front legs had started to atrophy. This meant that while she could still move her leg forward, the muscles she needed to pull the leg back in a walking motion were just too weak from the atrophy. It was time to stop using her cart for walks, but I continued to put her in her cart at meal times so she could stand up and eat. We had entered into the third stage of this disease.

Sassy was also getting fussier. Sometimes it was because she saw the cats, Zeek, or Buddy in her field of vision, and she didn't like being crowded. She had so little movement left that she was limited to barking and snapping her jaws at any animal that dared to come too close to her. She would sometimes try to bite me when I was moving her, or picking her up. I joked that she was part gremlin to lighten the mood, but I did not like seeing how distressed she became when she felt like her space was being invaded.

Other times she fussed because she was too hot, or needed to potty, or because she was uncomfortable and needed to be moved. Sometimes she seemed to fuss for no reason. She depended on me for almost everything now, and would watch me intently. When she needed help, she would make a soft noise to get my attention. I was at her beck and call.

> I used to be able to tell what my Boxer, Roxy, wanted by her actions. Now, after one and a half years of this awful disease, as she can only lay on her bed, I have to learn what she needs by the different whines/barks she makes! It's like learning a new language!
> —*Meredith*
> *Roxy, Boxer*

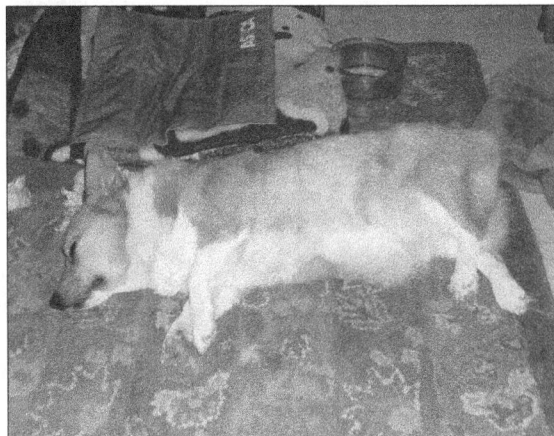

As her DM progressed, I didn't feel comfortable leaving Sassy for any length of time.

Friends offered to watch Sassy for me, but I was apprehensive about anyone else caring for her—even for a couple of hours. Of course, there were always times when I had to be away from her for short periods so I could go to the grocery store, doctor's appointments, or other errands.

I knew it was irrational, but I felt tremendous anxiety when I was away from her, almost to the point of having a panic attack. I carefully mapped out my errands so I could be extremely efficient and get back to her as quickly as possible.

It was becoming very hard to carry Sassy now—her body was flaccid from the shoulders back. It seemed like she lost her core strength very quickly, and she could no longer help hold herself up when I picked her up. It felt like I was picking up a sack of potatoes. I had to modify how I was picking her up so that I could support her torso as much as possible when I lifted her. When she needed to go potty, I would sit outside on a bench, and drape her body across my thighs, with her legs dangling on either side of my legs. I could then support her torso while I expressed her bladder and bowels.

Sassy had never been a very demonstrative or affectionate dog. She had a very independent personality, and I was surprised at how well she coped with me picking her up multiple times per day, helping her with everything except eating. I never felt that Sassy had bonded with me when I adopted her, but now that she was completely dependent on me, there was a growing bond between us. I was very tuned into her movements and her vocalizations, and for the most part, was able to read her cues about what she needed. She looked to me to take care of her, and she trusted me. We had a routine that worked well, and it felt like the schedule that I adhered to with Sassy provided a sense of safety for her. Our lives had become intricately bound together.

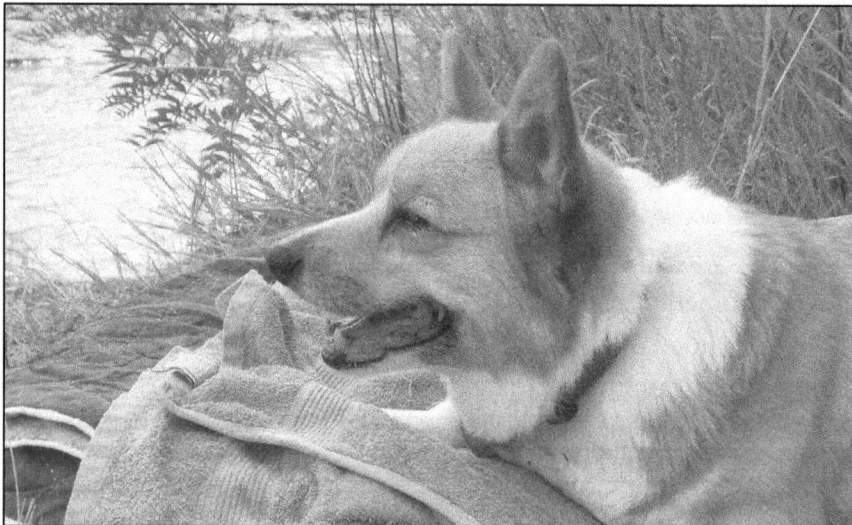

Enjoying a summer outing two years post onset of symptoms. Sassy is still a happy girl.

Another New Normal | Miriam Valere

Chapter Eighteen
Autumn changes

Sassy wasn't able to lift her head up very high anymore, and couldn't look over the sides of the wagon like she enjoyed doing. She was unbalanced in the wagon, and even with several folded-up blankets in it, she seemed uncomfortable. I knew that I needed to find a better solution for her. Several people in the DM groups had strollers for their dogs, so I started to look for one. In mid-September 2018, I checked the local classified ads one morning and saw a used dog stroller listed in almost brand-new condition, and for half the retail price. I quickly contacted the seller, and arranged to pick it up the next day.

This was such a wonderful gift for Sassy. It was long enough that her bed fit in it, and she could easily see out of the front. I always rolled up a towel or small blanket and put it in front of her neck so she could rest her head on it. It made going on walks much easier—the stroller was easy to push, and also wide enough that Buddy could ride in it with Sassy when he got tired.

It was obvious that Sassy really enjoyed the mental stimulation of riding in the stroller, so I took her out for rides often so she could enjoy the beautiful fall weather. Some days we just walked a few blocks for a quick outing before dinner, and when we had more time, we'd walk around the park or neighborhood. Sassy always slept deeply after one of our outings, so I know the fresh air and stimulation of seeing new sights was good for her.

Paying it forward

One day, I saw a post in the Corgi on Wheels group about a corgi named Fiona who was seal walking and needed a cart. I responded to that post saying that depending on Fiona's size, I had Sassy's Eddie's Wheels cart I could loan her. Fiona's mom, AnnaMarie, immediately sent me a message along with Fiona's measurements, and I saw Fiona was only off by about an inch on all the measurements. That made it close enough that I felt Sassy's cart could be adjusted to make it work.

I found out they lived about three hours from me, so I suggested we meet halfway, something they readily agreed to do. Based on the measurements

> When using the cart becomes hard for your DM baby, when their front end starts to get weak, remember to take them for stroller rides. Hallie perked up and enjoyed looking around for the whole ride. She smiled at me, happily woofed at Rusty walking next to her. Being outside enjoying the world gives them a wonderful new perspective.
>
> —*Michele Pierre*
> *Hallie,*
> *Pembroke Welsh Corgi*

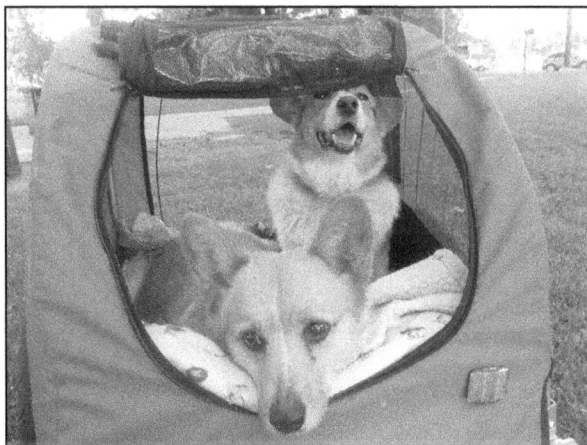

Sassy and Buddy enjoying their new stroller.

they had given me, I adjusted the cart, hoping that we'd be fairly close to the right fit for Fiona. The morning of October 21 was bright and clear, and I loaded all three dogs, plus both of Sassy's carts, into the car and we headed out. Once we found Fiona and her family at the park, I put Fiona in the cart to see where adjustments needed to be made. My initial adjustments were good—the length and the belly strap were the only areas that really needed to be addressed.

Fiona was a bit tentative the first time she walked with the cart. I did another adjustment, and put her back in the cart, showing AnnaMarie and her husband, Wes, how to put Fiona in the cart. It must have felt more comfortable to her, because this time she started walking right away, like she had always used the wheels. She gained confidence quickly as she realized she was no longer falling. I quickly found Fiona had stolen my heart. She was beautiful, sweet, and had that indomitable corgi spirit that I loved so much.

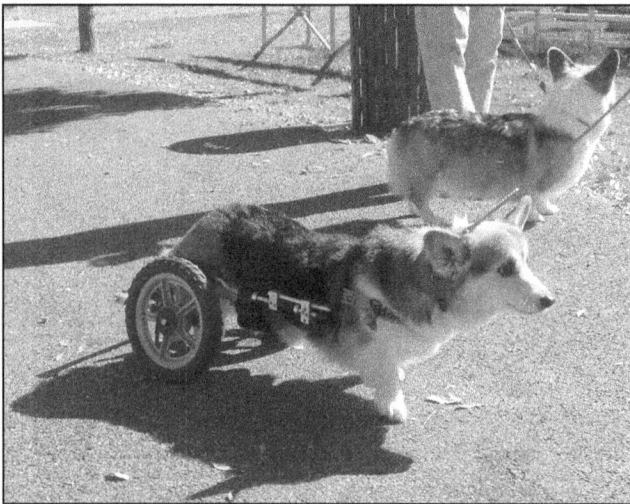

Fiona trying out Sassy's first set of wheels.

I had so many emotions watching her. Joy predominated, though there was a bit of lingering sadness in knowing that this was the end of a chapter in Sassy's life. But her original cart was needed by another dog now, and I wanted them to have the gift of mobility, just as Sassy had experienced.

To see Fiona, who was also blind, walk and even trot for a bit in the cart was heartwarming to me. I sent them on their way with tears in my eyes … so grateful and happy to be able to pay it forward and help another family in need. I knew Sassy's cart would serve Fiona until she no longer needed them, and then her cart would be passed on to yet another corgi in the future. These carts are practically indestructible, and I hope that many corgis will benefit from using Sassy's wheels.

A chance meeting

One Sunday afternoon, I was at the park with Sassy and the boys. I had several people stop to ask to pet the corgis. Our walk was taking much longer than I had planned, and the weather was turning cold, and looked like it might rain. I wanted to get home before it started to rain, as I didn't want Sassy to get chilled.

As we headed for the park entrance, I saw a stroller like Sassy's parked near the pond. A beautiful Boxer was laying in the stroller, and from her position, it looked like she was paralyzed. And if she was paralyzed, she probably had DM.

I walked up to the woman standing next to the stroller and said hello, and asked, "does your girl have DM?" The woman looked at me with surprise in her eyes, and I explained that my girl did as well. I introduced her to Sassy, and then to the boys, and she introduced me to her Boxer, Paige. We hugged each other, and both of us cried. There was a feeling of instant connection because we were both DM moms.

Paige and her mom were on vacation, and had stopped in Salt Lake City for a day to explore. They were leaving the city in a few hours. The chances of me being in that exact place at that exact moment to meet them seemed so unlikely—and I thought back to all the people who had "slowed" down our walk earlier by asking to pet the dogs. Without all those interruptions, I would have left the park at least thirty minutes earlier, and would have missed seeing Paige.

Meeting Paige, a Boxer with DM, at the park.

We talked—sharing tips, our achievements and joys, and also our fears. It was such a gift to run into someone coping with the same disease, and be able to talk in person.

That brief encounter made me realize just how isolated I felt in caring for a DM dog. While all my friends were supportive, and I knew a lot of people on social media with DM dogs, I didn't know anyone in my local community who was coping with caring for a DM dog. There was something very validating about having a face-to-face talk with someone who understood what Sassy and I were going through together.

An unexpected change

In mid-November I had a scare with Sassy. I kept a water dish next to her bed at all times, and was startled to realize that I had not seen her drink water for a couple of days. I searched through my memories of the past two days, hoping that I would remember something to indicate that she was still drinking water. I suddenly realized over the past couple of weeks I had been having more difficulty expressing her bladder. More accurately, I was having issues finding her bladder, and when I did, she didn't have as much urine as normal, and it was more concentrated. I berated myself. *How did I miss this? I should have been paying closer attention.* What that told me was she must have been slowly decreasing her intake of water for the last couple of weeks. I was horrified that I missed something so obvious. This could have caused some serious problems!

DM has moved into Sassy's front legs now. Note the position of her right front paw—she has lost the proprioception in that leg now.

I made some chicken broth for her, and added extra water to it, and she eagerly drank it and asked for more. That solved the immediate concern of her not getting enough water, but I needed to know why she wasn't drinking. I made a vet appointment with her for the next day so I could get her checked out. I was hoping that she had a UTI or some other explanation for this sudden change.

The vet did a thorough exam and ran a urinalysis, which came back as normal. There was no indication that she was sick in any way. I asked her vet if I should consider giving her subcutaneous fluids now, but it was recommended that I keep giving her watered-down broth. The vet also suggested that I add water to each of her meals.

As the vet did not find anything physically wrong with Sassy, I still had no idea why she wasn't drinking. I contacted my animal communicator, Valerie, and asked her if she could stop by to see Sassy. When she visited Sassy, she told me that Sassy felt scared to drink water. Valerie couldn't get a really clear message from Sassy, but got the sense that perhaps Sassy had choked when swallowing at some point, and now felt scared to try it again.

Another New Normal | Miriam Valere

Even though she was drinking the broth, because it smelled and tasted like food, it seemed to override Sassy's fear about liquid.

This approach rapidly improved the problems I had been having with locating her bladder. She was getting adequate fluids again, and I was able to easily feel her bladder again.

As we headed into December 2018, I knew in my heart that this would be Sassy's last Christmas—and last winter—with me. Sassy had so little movement remaining. She still had some strength in her left front leg, and could push herself a little with that leg, but it was minimal. If I held a treat over her head, she would lift her head to reach it, but without that motivation, she wasn't lifting her head much anymore. She was getting anxious more often. At night when I would put her in bed, she didn't settle down like she used to do. I started to sit next to her with my hand resting on her back until she fell asleep. Some nights it would take 45 minutes to an hour before she settled in to sleep. Fortunately, she was able to sleep all night still, and rarely would wake up before 7 AM. I was very grateful that I was still able to get a full night's sleep with her. So many people report that their DM dog is restless and barks much of the night, but somehow, we had managed to avoid that challenge.

I hoped that Sassy would make it until springtime, so she could enjoy sleeping in the grass again, but knew I couldn't take anything for granted right now. Now that we were so progressed into Stage 3 of DM, I knew she could flip into Stage 4, which was the final stage, without much warning.

Chapter Nineteen
January 2019

A few days after New Year's, Sassy's condition changed rapidly. She turned her head away from the broth I had been making her, and refused to take any liquids except for what little I mixed in with her food. If I added too much, she turned her head away from that too. I was worried.

I again contacted Dr. Coates at the University of Missouri and let her know that something had dramatically changed with Sassy. I asked her to send me the tissue collection kit, so that I could be prepared if Sassy declined rapidly. It was really important to me that I be able to donate tissue samples to the research studies—something good had to come from this experience. If by donating some of Sassy's tissues, it advanced the knowledge about DM even a small amount, then it felt like what we went through together was worthwhile. Knowing that the DM studies were also providing information for the studies about ALS made it all that more important to contribute her body to science when she died.

I felt awful thinking ahead and making plans for a necropsy when Sassy was still looking at me with alertness and interest in what was going on around her. I also knew that if I didn't get the logistics in place ahead of time, that I might end up in a crisis moment, and not be able to follow through with what was important to me. I wanted to get these details out of the way so I could focus 100 percent on Sassy in her last days—whenever those occurred.

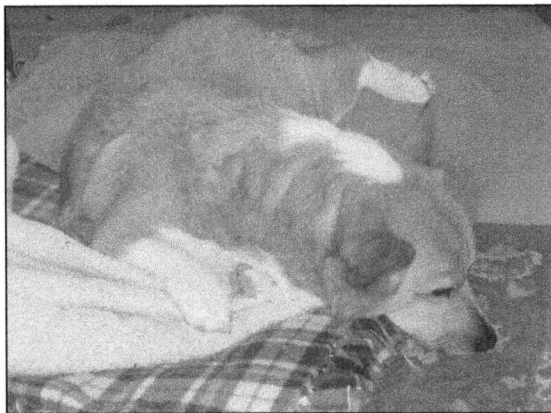

Sassy is very tired.

On Saturday, her breathing sounded labored, and had a raspy quality to it when she exhaled. I scrutinized her respiration rate. Sometimes it was normal, and other times it had increased. I wasn't sure what I was seeing. Was this the beginning of respiratory failure? My vet had indicated that a sustained increase in the respiration rate was a sign of distress, but what I was noticing was intermittent. Her eyes were bright, and her appetite still good, so I decided not to take her to the emergency vet for an evaluation unless her condition started to deteriorate more.

I contacted Tina and suggested that she come see Sassy as soon as she could. I felt that the end for Sassy might be really close, and I didn't want

Tina to miss out on the chance to see her one more time. It was an emotional visit—while Tina had visited Sassy periodically throughout the past year—the change in Sassy's appearance from her last visit was dramatic. It hit Tina very hard to see the dog she loved so much in such a state of decline. Tina left with tears in her eyes, expressing her heartfelt gratitude that I had given Sassy such a good home when she could no longer care for her. I assured her I would call her, day or night, if Sassy's condition deteriorated any more.

That night, I slept on the living room floor next to Sassy, with my hand on her side so I could feel any changes in her breathing overnight. Around 3:30 AM, her breathing improved, and she slept deeply the rest of the night. I offered a silent prayer, *Thank you, God, for allowing this little dog a respite. Thank you for easing her discomfort.*

On Sunday, her breathing had improved substantially, and she only had about an hour when it sounded labored. I was relieved, but didn't want to become complacent and think everything was OK. I knew that she could crash suddenly in full-blown respiratory failure. I watched her very closely all day, monitored her respiration rates, and rarely left her side.

Something has changed in her eyes … she's looking more worried.

I was able to get her in to see her vet on Monday, and after taking X-rays, it was determined that Sassy most likely had bronchitis. I had been so focused on end stage respiratory failure that I hadn't considered that maybe she was simply ill. We came home with ten days of antibiotics, and a request from the vet to recheck her in a week.

I received the tissue collection kit from Dr. Coates, and stored all the test tubes in the refrigerator as instructed, but did not read what was being requested. It felt rather morbid to think about what would happen during the necropsy, so I attempted to shield my mind from that as much as possible. When Sassy had her follow up appointment at the end of the week, her breathing had greatly improved, and I was relieved. I gave a copy of the tissue sample instructions to her vet and explained that I didn't think Sassy was quite ready to leave yet, but I wanted to have all the details worked out ahead of time. I knew we would have to schedule her euthanasia on a day when they would have time to do the necropsy and collect the samples.

This was unlike anything I had done before. Every other animal I had euthanized in the past had a sudden crisis that led to making the dreaded decision. With Sassy's condition, I knew it was best to set a date before that happened. Crisis for a DM dog at end stage meant organ or respiratory failure, and I wanted to be proactive and avoid that. It was difficult putting my emotions aside so I could take care of business—inside I was crying, and my heart ached anticipating the huge loss that was about to happen in my life. I had to hold it all together until I could get all the pieces lined up.

I felt a sense of relief that she had bronchitis, but also knew that this could be a sign that her lungs were becoming compromised. In my communications with Dr. Coates, she had explained that as DM progresses, the disease weakens the muscles of the chest wall, so they aren't able to get a full breath in and out. I didn't want Sassy to have bout after bout of respiratory illnesses, and realized that could be the outcome of having bronchitis. That wouldn't be fair to her.

Even though her breathing was improving, over the next few days, something had changed for the worse in Sassy's attitude. She seemed tired, or perhaps she was depressed. Her eyes took on a defeated look. Sassy started turning her head away from food now. I had to entice her to eat by offering new flavors of food—what she would eat in the morning, she'd refuse at dinnertime. I was using a syringe to squirt water inside her cheek to get fluids in her, since she still refused to drink the broth I made for her.

A member of the Corgis on Wheels group posted a profound question from a blog post she had found regarding quality of life issues and making the dreaded decision. It was simply this: *If your dog is not here tomorrow, what would she miss out on?*

That question stopped me in my tracks. I looked at Zeek and Buddy, and applied the question to them. They would miss out on walks, playing ball, chasing squirrels, meal times, learning new tricks, time with me … the list went on and on, as they both were actively engaged in life. When I applied the question to Sassy, the list was very short. She would miss having treats.

I knew it was time to let her go.

Honey dropped from 80 lbs. to 55 lbs. in a matter of months. She was 80 percent down in back. I carried her in and out of the house to do her business. She had basically stopped eating. The vet said to let her have anything that she would eat. I told Honey, "You let me know when it's time to go, because if it would be up to me, I would carry you in and out forever!" One day I carried her out and balanced her to do what she had to do and then I returned to the house to get my corgi puppy. When I returned, she was missing! I searched the area and found that she had dragged herself around to the front of the house and was lying under the rhododendrons. It was then that I knew she was telling me that she'd had enough and she was ready to go. I called and made the appointment.

—*Nancy Northrop*
Honey,
Husky/lab mixed breed

Making the call

I contacted Valerie, and asked her to check in with Sassy. The response from Sassy was that she was ready to go, but she would hold on until I was at peace with the decision. Valerie felt that I had less than two weeks to come to terms with this.

I started to contact friends, neighbors, and members of the local corgi group who were close to Sassy, and asked them to visit in the next few days if they wanted to say goodbye to her. It felt so strange to me to be making these preparations. When I've had animals in the past that needed to be euthanized, it had happened so suddenly, that there was no time to prepare, and no time to say goodbye. With Sassy, I was going to be able to plan it all out, and barring some crisis at the last minute, I'd be able to set a date to say goodbye.

Two days later, the vet's office called with disappointing news. They finally had a chance to look at what was being requested for the tissue samples, and they couldn't do it after all. They said that they didn't have the tools, or the skills, required to collect the type of samples that were now being requested. They had called the animal science department at Utah State University to see if they could assist, and they weren't able to either. My vet was very apologetic, but there just wasn't anything they could do.

Taking an outing to the park. This is how high she can lift her head now.

I was upset with this unexpected news. From the very beginning of learning about this disease, I was committed to helping research if I could, and it never dawned on me that the type of samples they needed would require specialized skills.

With this latest disappointment, there was no reason to delay my decision any longer. Sassy was ready, and I had to honor her needs. I decided that I would plan one last, fantastic week for Sassy, and let her have some special, normally forbidden food each day. At the end of that week, on January 20, I would have a vet come to the house to do an in-home euthanasia, and we would say goodbye. I let Tina know about the change in plans with the necropsy, and she agreed with me. It was time to say goodbye to Sassy.

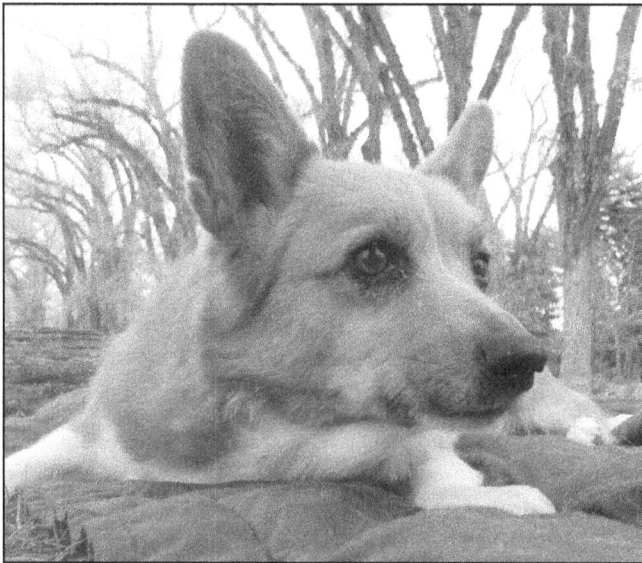

I spent some time searching on the internet for vets who did in-home euthanasia, and had a list of names to call, but I put it off for a couple of days. Even though I knew I had to make the call, I couldn't bring myself to do it just yet. It was so painful to think about when Sassy was still looking at me with bright eyes.

Since the weather was a little warmer, and Sassy had finished her course of antibiotics, I felt it would be safe to take her out in her stroller again. I wanted to be able to take Sassy out for stroller rides as often as possible to give her mental stimulation. Each day, I let Sassy have a special treat. So far, she had enjoyed steak, a grilled chicken breast, and some potato chips. I was careful to not give her so much to make her sick, and the treats made her meals more interesting, and gave her something to get excited about.

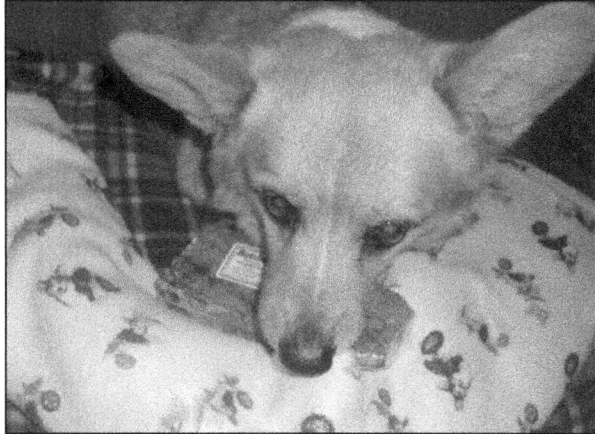

Sassy still has her enthusiasm for treats!

She looked brighter and happier than she had for the past few weeks, especially when Tiffany and Lauryn stopped by to see her. A few members of our local corgi group came for a visit; our group used to meet weekly, and Sassy always enjoyed the meet-ups—not to play with any of the dogs, but to spend time with all her favorite people. It was good for me to reconnect in person with these friends as well—we laughed together as we shared favorite memories of Sassy at the corgi meet-ups when she could still run. Everyone had similar stories about Sassy—her feisty personality, shamelessly begging for treats or belly rubs, and growling at all the other dogs.

Kismet

I misplaced the list I had made of vets to call, so had to do another online search to find the phone numbers again. As I was re-creating my list, for some reason I felt compelled to click on the "About" page of one of the vets I had found. To my astonishment, I read that this husband and wife vet team were involved in research and collaborating with vet schools on genetic disease research. It was a long shot, but I decided to send them an email and ask if they could do the necropsy and tissue collection. They responded later that day and asked for the list of what was needed, and I emailed it to them. I had a response the next day—yes, if they could get the tools they needed to handle this, they would be able to assist with the necropsy.

The only problem was they were at a conference for a full week, which meant that Sassy would need to hold on for another eight days. I had prepared myself to let her go on January 20, and now the earliest that this vet would be available was January 28. *Was I being selfish and too focused on the importance of the tissue donation?* I did not want to disregard Sassy's needs. *Would it be better to stick with my original plan and release her on Sunday?* There was no question in my mind that Sassy was ready to be set free. Her eyes had that faraway look in them that animals get when they're ready to depart their body. I've always thought when I've seen that "look" that they were somehow seeing what was on the other side of death, and liked what they saw. I didn't want Sassy to suffer because of my deep desire to help with the research study.

Using a syringe to give Sassy water.

Photo credit: Madison Briggs

I contacted Valerie again, and explained the situation. I was fully prepared to let Sassy go if she told Valerie that she couldn't wait any longer. I wasn't sure that this message could be conveyed adequately to explain the situation to Sassy, as a lot of animal communication is in pictures and feelings, and not words. Valerie's response was that Sassy clearly understood what I wanted to do, and she knew it was to ultimately help other dogs so they didn't have to go through what she did. Valere said that Sassy wanted to be part of that. Sassy told her that she would do her best to stay strong for a few more days. I thanked Sassy for her willingness to work with this unexpected delay.

I continued to focus on making Sassy's last few days as good as possible, and gave her as much love and affection as she would tolerate. However, she was starting to lose interest in eating her regular food. I was hand feeding her now, something I had said I would not put her through. It's one thing to hand feed and offer all kinds of food bribes to get a sick dog eating again when you expect a full recovery. It is a very different matter when you have a dog that is near end stage, whether that is with cancer, or some other disease. Sassy had always been food motivated, so to have her turn away from food told me that we didn't have a minute to spare. She was ready to leave her worn out body behind.

This was hard work, physically and emotionally. Sassy didn't seem to be suffering or in any obvious signs of distress … yet. However, I decided that if there were any signs of her becoming more uncomfortable, I would forego the tissue samples and let her go immediately. I couldn't ask her to give any more than what she had done already.

Counting the days

I was walking on eggshells—my normal routine felt like it was in a precarious balance that could change in a heartbeat. I watched Sassy closely for any signs that she was going into respiratory failure, or any other indication that she was suffering. After everything she had gone through, I could not let her suffer. I was feeling tremendous anxiety that this delay was going to be too much for her. I hadn't expected that she would be ready to go so quickly. Even though I had known for almost three weeks that the end was approaching, I thought we had at least a couple more months before it was time. It felt like I was going through heroics to get fluids in her and to get her to eat something each day—not for her benefit, but for mine. I questioned myself daily, and sometimes hourly, on whether I should skip the tissue donation so I could let Sassy go sooner.

Zeek was feeling the stress and uncertainty in the household. He had been self-crating himself on a regular basis, and was keeping his distance from Sassy. He was my canary in the coal mine (my personal advance warning system) and clearly showed me that there was too much stressful energy in the house. Zeek typically slept in the office while I worked—but for the past week he either stayed in the living room or slept in the hallway; always nearby, but not in the same room as Sassy. In the evenings, when Sassy and I would be in the living room, Zeek would stay in the kitchen.

I asked Valerie to stay in touch with Zeek, and to let him know why we were waiting to let Sassy go. She said he understood that Sassy would be leaving us soon. It was hard to watch the effect this was having on Zeek. I knew that after Sassy was gone, Zeek would benefit from some one-on-one time with me that I hadn't been able to give him for several months. Fortunately, Buddy didn't seem bothered by the events playing out in front of him. He was also enjoying the visitors who came to see Sassy, and happily snuggled with whomever would hold him during their visit.

I counted the days out on the calendar. We just needed to get through four days and a few more hours now … and then she could be at peace.

Shepherding a dog though DM is one of the toughest things I've ever done. It was also one of the most rewarding and I learned so much. If I could share one piece of advice it would be this one, shared to me by someone who's incredibly kind and wise: don't let your pup's worst day be her last day. That was my guide at the end. From a personal perspective I would suggest to DM parents that they not be hard on themselves. Because this disease is tough and we don't have many answers. Be as kind to yourself as you would be to another person having the same experience. And love your dog every single day. They feel and thrive on that love. My heart goes out to everyone impacted by this awful disease.

—*Angela Kalo*
Bailey,
Pembroke Welsh Corgi

I looked Sassy in the eyes each day, and told her how many more sunrises and sunsets we had left. I told her how brave she was being, and how honored I was to have been her caregiver during this time. I told her over and over how much I loved her. I hoped she somehow understood my words and the love I felt for her.

My emotions were frayed.

Friday

Our morning started rough. Sassy had a diarrhea accident when I got her up, so she needed a quick bath to start her day. She wasn't very interested in eating breakfast. I knew her tummy was most likely upset from all the different foods I had been giving her in an effort to get her to eat. She had a lot of gas, which I'm sure was making her uncomfortable. I massaged her abdomen, hoping to give her some relief. I couldn't get any fluids in her using the syringe—she just let it run out the side of her mouth, so I gave her subcutaneous fluids. I decided to not offer her any food for a few hours to let her system settle down. At dinner time, I opened yet another new flavor of food—and this time she was interested in eating and licked her bowl clean. I felt overwhelmed with gratitude for this small reprieve in the struggle. She slept comfortably all evening. That, too, was a gift.

Before I put her in bed for the night, I brought some water in a small bowl to her, with the syringe floating in it. I was just getting ready to syringe fluids in her, when she stuck her nose in the water, and started to drink on her own. That was the first time she had drunk any water on her own since November. I sat beside her, tears running down my cheeks. Another gift from my sweet girl.

Chapter Twenty
Saturday

This was the start of our last weekend together. The enormity of that hit me hard, but I was determined to focus on the joy of being together, and not let Sassy see me cry. I decided not to make any firm plans for the weekend, but to let our time together unfold as it needed to between visits with friends.

I took Sassy for a stroller ride to the park with a friend. I found a sunny place where the snow had melted, and put Sassy on her blanket, and let her enjoy being on the ground. Sassy was very alert, and enjoyed sniffing the thawing earth. When Sassy started to look tired, I put her back in her stroller and brought her home.

I had messages from two friends from the local corgi group wanting to visit, and both stopped by a couple hours later to sit with Sassy. Sassy's eyes were bright, and it was clear that she was enjoying the extra treats and love she was receiving. The three of us sat on the floor around Sassy, and she loved being the center of attention. It had been a long time since she had last seen these friends, and she seemed as happy as I was to spend time with them again. Sassy enthusiastically ate the sausage and egg bagel that was her special treat that afternoon.

It seemed to lighten the burden of what was coming soon to share that grief with others who loved Sassy, and to remember the fun times we used to have together when she was robust and active.

Later in the day, Tiffany came by to give Sassy a massage and to say goodbye. It was bittersweet, after so many months of providing therapy to Sassy, to know this would be her last time with Sassy.

After Sassy's last visitor of the day, she was very tired and slept soundly until dinnertime. Because she'd eaten some rich foods earlier in the day, I gave her kibble, not expecting her to be very interested, but she happily ate her entire bowl. She drank more water on her own throughout the evening. I felt such relief to have her drink on her own again.

Sassy seemed brighter-eyed and more interested in life that day than she had been for the past three

I made a promise to KC that we would only take this journey as long as she wanted to, and I was so grateful for every moment! When that day finally came, I held her in my lap like I did many, many times per day when she could no longer move herself or sit up. She crossed so very peacefully. When she had crossed Spenser (her companion dog) knew it—he knew it even before the vet did. He sat right next to KC, touching her until the very end. Once she had crossed, he got up, sniffed her, kissed her nose, and went to sit on his dad's lap. My husband took Spenser out to the waiting room to give me time to say goodbye. I had already said goodbye a thousand times, but I panicked at the thought of leaving KC alone in that room, even though she was gone. I know it was irrational, but I hadn't left her alone for over a year, not even to take a shower, and it felt so wrong to leave her alone now. I held her in my lap until a vet tech came to take her. Walking out of that room without KC was the hardest thing I've ever done.

—Tauni Beckmann,
#ShadeOutDM
KC, Pembroke Welsh Corgi

weeks. That was good to see. I hoped that tomorrow would be equally good. My heart felt at peace. I knew this was the right time to let her go. It felt good to be able to fill her last few days with fun activities and lots of visits from friends.

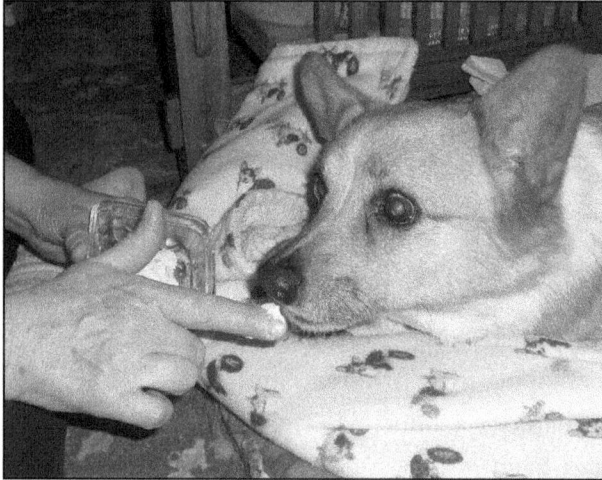

Whipped cream! That got her attention!

Sunday

Sunday was a quiet day, and it felt good to just sit and be quiet with Sassy. Tina wanted to have some one-on-one time with Sassy. She took Sassy out on a stroller ride at the park, but when they came back, Tina said she didn't think Sassy was very interested in being outside. Tina and I talked about what tomorrow would bring, and we cried together.

In the evening, Carrie, the person who first introduced us to the local corgi group, came over with a pepperoni pizza, and Sassy had a small piece for dinner. Sassy had always loved being with Carrie, and tonight was no exception. Carrie always hid treats in her coat pockets for Sassy to find, and it was fun to watch Sassy nose around, searching for the treats that she knew were there. Even with so little movement left in her body, she could still push with her nose and sniff out treats. I gave Carrie some time alone with Sassy to say her goodbyes.

As I went through all of our normal bedtime routines, I was acutely aware that this was the last time that I would tuck Sassy in bed for the night. The hours remaining felt sacred and precious. I had trouble falling asleep, and I listened to Sassy's slow, rhythmic breathing long into the night.

Sassy ready for bed on our last night together.

Chapter Twenty-One
The last day—January 28, 2019

Everything I did with Sassy carried the weight of knowing that I would never do that again with her.

I will never wake her up in the morning again.

I will never feed her breakfast again.

I will never brush her again.

I will never put her on her bed in my office again.

I will never reach over and pat her head while I am working again.

I will never carry her outside and express her bladder again.

I will never have to turn her over in her bed again.

I will never sit outside with her on a sunny day again.

I will never take another photo of her.

Sassy had all the special treats possible over the last week—steak, grilled chicken, potato chips, whipped cream, pizza, sausage and egg bagel, and a final meal of bacon, cheeseburger, a vanilla shake, and a Reese's Peanut Butter Cup for dessert. One final friend stopped by to say goodbye to her. Friends from around the world were sending her love to help her cross the Bridge in love and light. She was ready.

It was time.

Tina arrived at 2:00 PM with her partner, Sidd, and she stroked Sassy's soft fur, fed her treats, and told her how much she loved her.

Dr. Echols arrived at 2:30 PM. A brief neurological exam was

The last photo. My girl … my heart.

requested to be included with the tissue sample donation. Dr. Echols was very gentle with Sassy as he tested her reflexes, checked to see whether she had pain anywhere, and determined the level of paralysis she had. That exam took about 45 minutes, which gave Tina and me more time to give Sassy treats and love. Zeek and Buddy were sitting quietly nearby. They seemed to know what was going to happen, and didn't want to be close to Sassy.

After asking me if I was ready, Dr. Echols gave Sassy an injection of a deep sedation drug so she would be unconscious. It was so hard to watch her slowly fade into a deep sleep—but I took comfort that her last memories were of being loved and eating her favorite treats.

One final step of the exam remained, and that was to collect two vials of blood to send with the tissue samples. Dr. Echols had suggested that Sassy be sedated before he drew those samples, so that she wouldn't experience any pain, and I felt like that was a sensible plan.

Dr. Echols shaved one leg, and couldn't find a good vein. Then another leg—and that vein blew out as soon as he inserted the needle. He explained that one of the side-effects of paralysis is that the vein quality deteriorates, making it difficult to do a blood draw. I suggested that maybe we should skip this step if it was going to be too difficult, but he felt he could do the blood draw from her neck. He shaved some fur off her neck, but still couldn't find a good vein to pull blood from, so he said he'd try on the other side. My heart was full of despair as he turned her over and started to shave the other side of her neck. Even though I knew she wasn't aware of what was going on, it was devastating to see her beautiful fur being shaved off. I didn't want this to be my last memory of Sassy.

A gift from Sassy

But just as suddenly as I had that thought, it was replaced with a glorious scene from the C. S. Lewis book, *The Last Battle*. In that story, there is a scene where the hero of the story, Aslan the Lion, is captured and tied down. His captors shaved his beautiful mane in an attempt to make a mockery of him before they killed him. As the story continues, during the night, the mice and other little creatures chewed through the ropes that bound their dead hero. As dawn broke, Aslan rose from the dead in his full glory, bigger, and more magnificent than before.

That was a book I had not thought about in at least thirty years, and there was no way that image came unbidden to me. I know without any doubt that Sassy sent me that image to comfort me, and to tell me that she would be whole again as soon as she crossed over the Rainbow Bridge.

Dr. Echols finished the blood draw, and he looked at me for permission to inject the final drug. I quickly looked at Tina to make sure she was ready, and then nodded, tears streaming down my face. Sassy's breathing increased for a few breaths, and then stopped.

It was over.

My beautiful girl was free of the body she had been trapped in.

Running free

After helping Dr. Echols carry Sassy's body to his car on a stretcher, I sent Valerie a text message that Sassy was gone. Her reply from Sassy was almost immediate:

Mommy, Mommy … I forgot how much I love to run! And I can breathe!

Chapter Twenty-Two
Life after DM—February 25, 2019

It's been almost a month since Sassy left my side. I miss my girl. There is a big empty place that she used to occupy. Spending the past two and a half years caring for her, with the last year having our lives so intricately bound up in each other, my every waking moment caring for her, or checking her to see if she needed me … it feels like I'm forgetting to do something important. I keep listening for her little noises that mean she needs to go potty, or that she is too hot, or that she needs something else. I am acutely aware of her absence.

Surprisingly, I don't feel grief-stricken about Sassy's death. I realize grieving is a unique journey for each person, and even how I grieve for different animals has varied greatly over the years. Sassy gave me such a beautiful gift as she was slipping free of her body, that it feels like my time with her was complete. The finality of letting her go was devastating, of course. There is simply no way to watch a loved one die in front of you and not be deeply affected by that experience.

I am left with a feeling of peace. I know that her spirit is free now, no longer bound by the constraints of that tired, old body that she was trapped in. That is a gift to be cherished. Of course, I still get blindsided by sadness and tears. A couple of days ago, I put on a jacket I hadn't worn for several months, reached in the pocket and found one of Sassy's booties. Something so simple … and I was in tears. I may not be engulfed with grief on a day-to-day basis about Sassy, but waves of sadness continue to flow through me. I miss her. I miss listening to her breathe at night. I miss how she smells. I miss her attitude.

Paying it forward, again

I saw a video of a corgi being pulled on a sled in the snow, and had a gut feeling that she had DM. I contacted her owner and asked if they were going through that, and if so, did they need a wheelchair for their girl. The answer to both questions was *"yes,"* so I boxed up Sassy's cart and sent it to Daisy to use. It felt good to be able to help another family with a DM baby gain some mobility.

> On the day your DM dog flies to the Rainbow Bridge you will suddenly become aware that your arms are now empty. It's something you won't be prepared for and something you never thought about until they are gone. We become their legs. We lift them and carry them and hold them. They become a physical part of our being and I had no idea how great that bond was until the day Denby flew to the bridge. I told him, "DM may have broken and damaged your body but your heart and spirit were always perfect in my eyes." It took time before I could fold his blanket and leave it behind.
>
> —*Denise & Denby,*
> *Pembroke Welsh Corgi*

Daisy received Sassy's K9 cart.

Simple gifts

I am experiencing the simple gift of having more hours to myself each day. My normal morning routine—walking Zeek and Buddy, feeding all my animals, cleaning litter boxes, getting ready for work, eating breakfast—used to take me at minimum two hours to accomplish, and now only takes 45 minutes. I am able to focus for longer than twenty minutes at a time without interruptions, which is making me more productive with my work.

I can feel layers of stress rolling off my body. I am sleeping more deeply. Taking a shower feels luxurious now—I don't need to be on high alert listening for Sassy's bark, anxious that she can't see me. I can take my time doing errands. I can take Zeek and Buddy on long walks, and not have to hurry home.

I see the transformation in Zeek. He is smiling again and playing more. Since Frodo died, Zeek did not want to walk with me alone. Now that Sassy is gone, Zeek enjoys taking long walks with me again. I realize now that he was concerned about Sassy, and didn't want to leave her alone.

There is also a sense of relief that now I can focus on finding yet another new normal—but one with more stability and a focus on simply living a regular, routine life that does not revolve around the full-time care of a family member.

July 2019—six months later

My calm acceptance of losing Sassy in January has shifted to feelings of anger that I had to lose her prematurely to this awful—and preventable—disease. She was otherwise healthy, and while I can't predict what her life expectancy would have been without DM, I can say with all certainly that had she not had this horrible disease, she would have lived her last few years of life with the ability to move on her own … to have the freedom to follow me around the house … to wander where her nose took her on walks … to be able to roll over, and sleep on her back … to scratch an itch with her hind leg … to be as active as she wanted to be. DM stole all of that from her.

The waves of grief roll in and out of my awareness on an almost daily basis now. Each time I hear of another dog losing the DM battle, the pain of losing Sassy rises to the surface again. Several of the dogs that were highlighted in quotes throughout this book, and many more in the DM community have died in the last six months. I feel a deep sadness, and cry for each one of those dogs as I get the news of their death—and as I grieve, I feel another layer of my own pain come to the surface to be released.

Right now, it's like my grief is covered with a thin scab that is constantly getting broken open with each dog that dies, never getting the chance to totally heal before the next death occurs. But I think this is also cathartic for me, and part of my own healing process. I have always struggled with expressing my feelings, and in the process of allowing myself to feel pain for the loss of another dog, my grief is getting acknowledged as well. I know that time will eventually ease the pain of loss, and the tears won't spill out so quickly. There will be a day when the heavy curtain of grief will fall to the side, and the happy memories of the time we had together will be all that remains.

Despite my tears and grief, I am at peace with my decision to let her go. I know without question that Sassy was ready to end her struggles with her paralyzed body. I know I did everything possible to keep her happy and healthy through the two and a half years that we coped with DM.

I am honoring Sassy's life in the words of this book. I hope that by sharing this journey—her story—her memory will live on. To you who may be just starting on this journey, I wish you peace of heart, and encourage you to find joy in the smallest of moments with your beloved companion. I hope that some part of this story will resonate with you, and that you will be able to cope better because of something I have written.

The way I coped with this disease was to learn from Sassy about how to stay in the present moment. That was such an incredible gift to be able to slowly start to see the world through her eyes. She handled being paralyzed with dignity, and up until the last three weeks of her life, she was extremely happy. I'll never know for sure what created the change that occurred in early January with her—perhaps it was a combination of being 14 years old, having DM, and developing bronchitis that just was too much for her compromised body. Perhaps she was heading into end stage organ failure, or perhaps she had some other illness that I was unaware of. Regardless of the cause, she made it abundantly clear to me that she was ready to leave my side, and I am grateful that I had become so tuned into the nuances of her expressions and movements that I understood the message that she was giving me.

I tested Zeek for the DM mutation a year ago, and he is a carrier, so I will not have to go through this with him. I just received Buddy's test results, and he is At Risk. While I don't know if Buddy will develop the disease, I know that what I learned from going through this with Sassy will help me if he does. I hope that I won't have to face DM again, but I no longer dread hearing a toenail scrape during a walk, or seeing a wobble and a misstep. I am stronger, and more compassionate from having been on this journey with Sassy. That was her gift to me.

This disease is cruel, heartbreaking, and unlike any disease I have ever encountered in caring for an animal. When you have a dog with cancer, kidney disease, heart disease, or any number of other illnesses—you know without any doubt that your dog is sick. You know the path is going to be about managing symptoms until your dog becomes so ill that there is no question that it is time to set them free because they are in pain and suffering. DM is not like that at all. Your DM dog is going to be healthy, alert, interested in everything going on around them, right up until their last breath— the last breath that you have to decide when will happen. The only thing that is wrong is your dog cannot move at all, except for limited movements in their front legs and their neck if you've let the disease advance to the end of its progression. It is so hard to make that call to your vet to schedule the day, when your dog is not sick in the usual sense. For people who are caring with the large breeds prone to DM, the decision to euthanize is even harder. Most people with the large breeds make the decision when their dog has lost use of their hind legs—not because they are unwilling to care for them any longer, but because they aren't physically

Our final family portrait, a week before Sassy crossed the Bridge. Sassy is still very alert mentally, but is trapped in her body and only has limited movement of her neck and head.

Another New Normal | Miriam Valere

able to lift their partially paralyzed dog and support their weight while they potty, or even to lift them into a wheel chair. They are cheated out of at least a year, maybe two years of time with their beloved companion, simply because their dog is too heavy to pick up.

From a caregiving perspective, caring for a DM dog is incredibly difficult. Even as a child, I was a caregiver, always wanting to heal and fix any animal that was sick or injured. With that as my personality, I have learned over the years how easy to it is to get lost in the process of caring for another, and how important it is to take care of yourself during the journey. But caring for a DM dog is unlike anything that I have ever experienced. Looking back, the first year with Sassy was relatively easy from a physical perspective. She was still able to walk on her own for several months from first onset of symptoms, and then could walk with the assistance of a cart.

Emotionally, it was a really hard year coming to terms with what was going to happen to her. Once I made peace with the emotional aspect of caring for a handicapped dog, the physical challenges increased during our second year of coping with DM. Without really realizing what was happening, I became so immersed in the process of taking care of Sassy that it dominated my entire life. As she became increasingly dependent on me to help her, she became my focal point, so much so that being away from her created tremendous anxiety in me. Could I have left her more often? It is likely that she would have been able to handle me being away from her more often for short periods of time—but the fear that she needed something prevented me from doing that. When I knew that she didn't have the ability to even scratch an itch, or to shift her position, I just couldn't leave her.

No dog should have to live out its senior years paralyzed from a **preventable** disease. I hope that Sassy's story will help educate others about the perils of this genetic disease that can be eradicated with good breeding practices.

This disease must be stopped.

Chapter Twenty-Three
The truth about degenerative myelopathy

In 2008, Dr. Coates, and the other researchers at the University of Missouri discovered mutations in the canine SOD1 gene, the same gene mutation that in humans can cause amyotrophic lateral sclerosis (ALS). This genetic mutation causes degeneration in the white matter of the spinal cord. The white matter is involved with transmitting the movement commands from the brain to the legs.[6]

> *Degenerative myelopathy of dogs, also called chronic degenerative radiculomyelopathy, is a slowly progressive, noninflammatory degeneration of the axons and myelin primarily affecting the white matter of the spinal cord. It is most common in German Shepherds, Pembroke Welsh Corgis, Boxers, Rhodesian Ridgebacks, and Chesapeake Bay Retrievers, but is occasionally recognized in many other breeds. The cause is a mutation in the superoxide dismutase1 (SOD1) gene, inherited in an autosomal recessive pattern with incomplete penetrance. It is similar to familial amyotrophic lateral sclerosis in human patients. Pathologically, there is noninflammatory degeneration of axons in the white matter of the spinal cord, which is most severe in the thoracic region.*
>
> *Affected dogs are usually >8 yr. old and develop an insidious onset of nonpainful ataxia and weakness of the pelvic limbs. Spinal reflexes are usually normal or exaggerated, but in advanced cases there is flaccid tetra paresis and hyporeflexia reflecting lower motor neuron involvement. Early cases may be confused with orthopedic disorders; however, proprioceptive deficits are an early feature of degenerative myelopathy and are not seen in orthopedic disease. . . .*
>
> *There is no specific treatment and no evidence that glucocorticoids, other drugs, or supplements alter the course of the disease. Most dogs are euthanized because of disability within 1–3 yr. of diagnosis.[7]*

That is the scientific cause of degenerative myelopathy. But the sad truth is, this genetic disease is proliferated by bad breeding practices in over 100 different breeds. Boxers, German Shepherds, and Pembroke Welsh Corgis are all breeds that have a high percentage of DM present in the gene pool.

Breeding best practices

Prior to 2008, breeders didn't have the ability to determine if their bloodlines carried the DM gene. But today, for less than $65, you can easily test your dogs in the comfort of your home with a simple cheek swab DNA kit. Breeders can make decisions to breed their dogs carefully to slowly

6. ibid [5]

7. Thomas , W. B. "Degenerative Diseases of the Spinal Column and Cord." *Merck Manual Veterinary Manual.* Accessed April 19, 2019 through https://www.merckvetmanual.com/nervous-system/diseases-of-the-spinal-column-and-cord/degenerative-diseases-of-the-spinal-column-and-cord#v26305110

eliminate the gene from their bloodlines. Statistically, here is what happens in different breeding scenarios:

- Both parents are Clear, then all puppies will be Clear.
- If one parent is a Carrier and the other is a Clear, then about 50% of the puppies will be Carriers and 50% will be Clear.
- If both parents are Carriers, then about 25% of the puppies will be Clear, 50% will be Carriers, and 25% will be At Risk.
- If one parent is Clear, and the other At Risk, then all the puppies will be Carriers.
- If one parent is a Carrier and the other parent is At Risk, then about 50% of the puppies will be Carriers, and 50% will be At Risk.
- If both parents are At Risk, all the puppies will be At Risk.

Visual of breeding risk factors.

DM Breeders Chart

Parents		Statistical Predisposition			
Clear	Clear	100% Clear			
Clear	Carrier	50% Clear		50% Carrier	
Clear	At Risk	100% Carrier			
Carrier	Carrier	25% Clear	50% Carrier	25% At Risk	
Carrier	At Risk	50% Carrier		50% At Risk	
At Risk	At Risk	100% At Risk			

It's important to note that having an At Risk result on a DNA test does not mean your dog will definitely develop the disease. Researchers do not know yet what turns the gene on allowing the disease to manifest. Carriers will most likely never develop DM (there are a few rare instances where a carrier has developed DM, but the majority of dogs with DM carry both copies of the mutation). Over time, using genetic testing and selective breeding could eliminate degenerative myelopathy from the gene pool.

Currently, statistics from the OFA show that out of 3,815 Pembroke Welsh Corgis tested for DM, 53.4% tested At Risk, and 34% tested as Carriers. With almost 90% of the breed carrying at least one copy of this gene, it's readily apparent why all corgis need to be tested before breeding.[8]

Of course, there are many other genetic diseases that need to be taken into consideration when breeding dogs. Responsible breeders focus on preserving the genetic diversity in the breed, along with the best qualities of

8. Orthopedic Foundation for Animals (OFA). "Breed Statistics." Accessed May 5, 2017 through https://www.ofa.org/diseases/breed-statistics?disease=DM

Another New Normal | Miriam Valere

that particular breed. Temperament, structure, conformation, hip dysplasia, vision and hearing issues, are among just a few of the things that a breeder needs to take into consideration when breeding dogs. The ultimate goal of every breeder should be to **improve** the breed, and produce a quality dog that can be an excellent companion, pet, or service animal.

On the surface, this seems like something all breeders would be focused on—but that is far from the truth. There are hundreds, if not thousands, of "backyard" breeders who see the dollar signs associated with selling puppies. When a purebred puppy can command a price of $1,500 or more, those eager to make some "easy" money on the side decide that they will breed their dog. They rationalize that their dog is registered through the American Kennel Club (AKC) so that must mean their dog is a quality dog; but for breeding purposes, that registration is essentially meaningless. The only thing that having an AKC registered dog means is that both parents of that dog were purebred and registered with the AKC. It does not guarantee that the dog is healthy, has good genes, or a good temperament. So, in ignorance (and in greed), they breed … and then sell those innocent puppies to unsuspecting buyers who are equally ignorant about the genetics of the breed they are buying.

Even worse are the puppy mills that keep their dogs in horrific conditions and mistreat the breeding stock, frequently not even providing vet care, clean conditions, or protection from the weather. They turn around and sell the puppies to pet stores, and again, the unsuspecting buyer is captivated by the adorable puppy, not knowing that their life may very well be turned upside down because of health issues resulting from bad breeding.

And sadly, there are professional breeders who are not concerned with breeding dogs who carry the degenerative myelopathy gene, because they see it as a "old-age" disease. They argue that it is equally devastating having your dog die of cancer or kidney disease. They cite statistics indicating that even if a dog is At Risk, it may not develop the disease, so why worry about it? Or they tout the fact that the disease doesn't cause pain, so it really won't bother your dog that much if they develop it. They rationalize their refusal to test and breed out the DM gene, saying it would restrict the gene pool too much, resulting in even more genetic diseases that occur with inbreeding.

There is some truth in that last statement if the focus is 100% on eliminating the DM gene and not being aware of the other genetic diseases. However, responsible breeding has been proven to work in producing healthy, DM

After 2009, when DNA testing became available, the process to eliminate DM in breeding programs should have started. There is no reason on earth reputable breeders should ever have to produce a DM AT RISK puppy ever again. By selective breeding, and investing in quality DM clear stock, over time, a breeder can eliminate the At Risk mutation from their lines. I'm a previous owner of two DM Corgis—a Pembroke and a Cardigan. In the past, I successfully bred & showed Collies, finishing many champions so I know both sides this issue. Every single puppy I bred was health tested for the genetic diseases.

—*Pamelia Brown,
former breeder
Sasha, Cardigan Welsh
Corgi and Teddy,
Pembroke Welsh Corgi*

DM is a horrible disease, that results in heart break for the owner and their dog. With a simple $80 test, we can work to eliminate that disease in the puppies we produce. In our breeding program, we do panel testing for a wide variety of genetic diseases in addition to DM, such as MDR1, which causes intolerance to certain common medications like Ivermectin. We also focus our breeding program for temperament which is also genetic, as dogs with anxiety and other temperament concerns can become aggressive. Though there are several diseases that I test for, DM is a top priority.

It's important to me to work to only produce DM CLEAR puppies for the sake of the owner, and the breed. With the gene pool small in certain breeds, it takes time to eliminate the DM gene, but if you breed an At Risk with a Clear, you will produce carriers, which in most breeds will never develop DM. Breeding Carriers to Clears will produce a percentage of carriers. But you never should breed a Carrier to Carrier, or an At Risk to Carrier, because then you are producing At Risk puppies. Unless you test your breeding stock, you won't know which dogs are Carriers or At Risk.

I have a friend who unknowingly bought a puppy from a backyard breeder. She didn't have much money or knowledge and decided to trust this breeder. She needed a service dog to start training. Her livelihood and life depended on it. Sadly, a couple years later she had her service dog tested for DM—this is a dog she has spent thousands of hours training and building a bond with—and her dog tested At Risk for DM. While her dog may not develop DM, her owner now has the fear of an unknown future for her best friend. One simple, inexpensive test could have prevented this heartache of worry and wondering if her service dog is going to become disabled.

All it takes is one test. There is no excuse as a breeder to not test.

—*Taylor Mietl, breeder*
Lost Creek German Shepherds

free bloodlines and champion dogs. These efforts are creating more diversity and healthier dogs.

While I agree that cancer and other diseases are devastating, there is no DNA test available to determine risk factor for those diseases—but there is for DM. To have the means to determine if your breeding stock carries a serious fault like DM, and not test for it is inexcusable. I cannot fathom someone saying they love a particular breed, and not care whether they are producing pups that may be stricken with this horrific disease; for a breeder to take that stance is unethical and cruel, in my opinion. I don't know what kind of wake-up call it will take for these breeders to understand the harm they are doing to innocent dogs who deserve to live out their senior years unencumbered by a wheelchair, not to mention the stress and physical demands placed on the caregiver of that dog.

What can be done?

If you are determined to buy a puppy, educate yourself about the breed. Do your research about the qualities of that breed, their personality, and what health issues the breed is prone to. The Orthopedic Foundation for Animals (see *Resources*) is an excellent resource to understand the health issues in different breeds. If you know the AKC registration number of a dog, or the kennel name it came from, you can search the OFA database to see what health testing has been done through the OFA.

Don't decide to buy a puppy simply because it is "cute" or the popular breed of the year. Do your research! Make sure that the breed matches your temperament and lifestyle. If you live in a small apartment in the city, and prefer binge-watching

Netflix over going outside for long walks, don't get an active breed like a herding dog. I blame the high percentages of DM in the corgi breed to their popularity—too many people want a corgi simply because it is so cute to look at—which has led to so many puppy mill situations with this breed. Not only are those unethical people breeding more dogs carrying the DM gene, but they are also breeding for bad temperament, poor conformation, and a whole list of other health issues in the corgi breed.

Research breeders. Join breed specific groups on Facebook or other social media sites and ask who the good breeders are. Follow up by asking people who have dogs from specific breeders what their puppies are like. When you contact your list of breeders, ask questions about the health testing they have done. Be prepared to be on a wait-list for a quality puppy, and pay a premium price for that healthy puppy.

Backyard breeders and puppy mills can be shut down if people stop buying the puppies. Like everything, it's a simple supply-and-demand equation that keeps those people in business. If the demand decreases, eventually they will stop breeding as it is no longer profitable. When enough people start asking questions about genetic testing when calling on an ad for available puppies, and then say *"No, thank you"* when they find out the dogs haven't been health tested, the backyard breeders will be forced to either start breeding responsibly, or give it up. Given that it is very time consuming and expensive to be a quality breeder, most backyard breeders will give it up.

If you truly love a particular breed, then be a responsible buyer, educate yourself, and only buy from quality breeders. If you're like me, and prefer to rescue dogs, you will never have the ability to choose a DM clear dog as your next dog, and you'll have to be prepared to love, and care for that dog, no matter what happens later in their life. You still have a voice to help educate others though, so spread awareness whenever you can about DM.

How is degenerative myelopathy diagnosed?
Getting a diagnosis of degenerative myelopathy is a process of elimination, complicated by the fact that many vets have never worked with a DM dog before. There are other diseases and injuries that can initially cause similar neurological changes that occur with DM, so typically a vet will want to do X-rays at the minimum, and possibly an MRI to rule out a spinal injury, disc disease, other neurological disorder, or a spinal tumor.[9]

9. Canine Genetic Diseases Network (CGN). "Degenerative Myelopathy–Disease Basics." Accessed February 12, 2017 through http://www.caninegeneticdiseases.net/dm/basicdm.htm

10. Bush Veterinary Neurology Service (BVNS). "Degenerative Myelopathy (DM)." Accessed July 2, 2019 through https://bvns.net/degenerative-myelopathy/

One of the main hallmarks of DM is there is no pain associated with it; your dog simply loses coordination (ataxia) of one hind leg, and then the other, and becomes fully paralyzed in the hind legs. If your dog lives long enough, he will become paralyzed in his front legs as well. This is called *tetraparesis.* The progression of DM is slow, with several months between first onset of symptoms to paralysis of a rear limb.

Sometimes a vet will recommend putting your dog on an anti-inflammatory medication for 7-10 days as part of the process of elimination. If there is improvement in your dog's gait and coordination, then an injury causing inflammation is suspected. With a DM dog, there will be no change in gait, or any improvement of symptoms from medications.

If your dog is showing ataxia in one hind leg only, there is no pain involved, and X-rays or MRI show a normal spine, then a presumptive diagnosis of DM is given. Using the DNA test and determining your dog is A/A (Abnormal/Abnormal or At Risk) is helpful information for your vet to make this diagnosis. If you were to receive DNA results of N/N (Normal/Normal or Clear) or N/A (Normal/Abnormal or Carrier), then what you're seeing with your dog is almost certainly not degenerative myelopathy, and may be treatable.

The only way to confirm the presumptive diagnosis is post-mortem with a necropsy to examine the spinal cord under a microscope. DM causes degenerative changes in the spinal cord that are not typical of any other neurological disease.

But for the many people who are caring for a DM dog, a necropsy isn't necessary to confirm the diagnosis. There is no doubt in our minds about what we are dealing with.

The stages of DM
DM follows a typical pattern of progression in most dogs. It's important to note that not all dogs will experience every one of these symptoms.[10]

Stage 1
First onset of symptoms. You may notice weakness in one hind leg, decreased coordination, difficulty making the transfer from lying down (or sitting) to standing, or not being able to navigate stairs. These symptoms are also seen with common conditions like arthritis, hip dysplasia and other spinal issues, such as a herniated disc, which is why consulting a neurologist, and getting X-rays and an MRI are so important.

Stage 2

As the disease progresses, you may see your dog knuckling on their hind paw, crossing of the hind legs under the body, or dragging a hind leg. You'll notice more toe nail wear on the two middle toes. If your dog has a tail, it may be limp now. You will possibly notice a hoarseness or loss of volume when your dog barks. You may feel that symptoms seem to plateau for a while, and then suddenly see big changes happening overnight. There may be a time period when your dog cannot stand on its own, but can "seal walk." Soon after that phase, your dog may not be able to sit upright. Urinary and/or fecal incontinence may start to occur late in this stage for most dogs. As this stage progresses, your dog will lose function of both hind legs.

Stage 3

Your dog is fully "down" in the back now, and is paralyzed in both hind legs. You will start to see more noticeable muscle atrophy in the hind legs and hips now. Urinary and/or fecal incontinence is most certainly occurring now. You may have to cope with pressure sores developing over bony areas, as your dog cannot move enough on its own now to relieve the pressure in those areas. It's important at this

A breeder has many, many other issues to consider than just DM. Throwing out quality carriers and at risk/affected dogs just because of such tight focus on a single disease would be disastrous. In Pembroke Welsh Corgis, there is a long history of vonWillebrand's Disease Type I. It's a blood clotting disorder that starts when a dog is two or three years old. Breeders had bred it almost entirely out of Pembrokes, but it's on the rise because many casual or commercial breeders are only testing for DM, because that's what the public sees as the greatest health concern in the breed. How about Exercise Induced Collapse? Usually shows up by 1st birthday, and can be fatal. Recently confirmed in Pembrokes, although previously mostly associated with Sporting Group breeds, but also seems to be rising. Eye issues: PPM (Persistent Pupillary Membrane), PRA (Progressive Retinal Atrophy) and juvenile cataracts can all run in families, all problematical for the life of the dog. Want your Pembroke to look like a Pembroke? You need to choose good type. No one wants to deal with hip dysplasia, elbow dysplasia, patellar luxation … are DM clear dogs all free of these? And let's not forget the importance of temperament! There is clear evidence both parents, but especially the dam, contribute a great deal to puppy temperaments.

Purebred dog gene pools are already very tight, often having fewer than 20 individuals that started the lines. Keeping as much genetic diversity as possible helps maintain the breed with the best chance of breeding out of a "corner" and decreasing incidences of disease(s)/mutations that may be worse and harder to get rid of in the future. Breeding DM clear to at risk/affected means all puppies will be carriers - at no greater risk of developing DM than a clear dog. The best DM carrier(s) from that mating, bred to DM clear, gives both clears and carriers. And a bloodline and features are preserved. But all other testing must also be done. In my most recent litter from a DM clear male to DM carrier female mating, I got four DM clear puppies, and two carriers, out of the litter of six. Three of those were clear for both DM and vWD1, and one of those remains with me with the hopes of breeding the next generation. Because I take all genetic testing into consideration when making mating selections, as well as all the other factors I mentioned, no one is buying an at risk/affected DM, vWD1 and/or EIC puppy from me. And I've done everything I can to perpetuate breed type with excellent temperaments, and minimize risk of other health concerns.

—*Kimberley Harvey, breeder*
Dragonsdale Corgis

stage to turn your dog every 4-6 hours to help prevent pressure sores. Your dog will lose core strength, and you'll see weakness in the front legs. The disease progression is more rapid now. As the disease progresses, your dog will be unable to stand or walk, even in a wheeled cart. Your dog will still be able to move his head, but will no longer be able to push himself into an upright position at all. He may not be able to remain on his belly without a rolled towel to support him in that position. Frequently dogs in this stage will develop urinary tract infections, as it is difficult for them to fully empty their bladder. Your dog may be developing anxiety at this stage. Many DM dogs exhibit "sundowner" behavior where they become increasingly anxious as the evening light fades. This can be very difficult to cope with for both the caregiver and their dog.

Stage 4/End stage

The last stage of this disease is progression to the brain stem. The cranial nerves become damaged from the disease, which can lead to respiratory issues. Breathing issues are always an indication that your dog is suffering, and needs to be considered a medical emergency. It is not advised to let your dog progress into the later stages of end stage, as there are multisystem failures as the kidneys, lungs, heart and other organs fail.

The importance of a necropsy

One of the many challenges of DM is the inability to confirm diagnosis of the disease in a living dog, as the DNA test only shows risk factor, not whether your dog will actually develop DM. Without a necropsy to confirm the presumptive diagnosis, we'll never know for sure how many dogs are affected by this disease, nor will we know what percentage of At Risk dogs actually go on to develop the disease. While researchers can extrapolate statistics from the data they currently have, there are still a lot of unknowns with this disease. The more necropsies that can be performed to confirm the diagnosis, the more information researchers will have about DM and how prevalent it is in different breeds. However, what we do know with full certainty is there are too many dogs ending up in wheelchairs in their senior years.

But choosing to have a necropsy done on your dog is challenging. Emotionally, it can be very painful to think about donating your beloved dog's body to science, so many people opt not to do this. It can also be very expensive, making a heartbreaking time more difficult by the added stress of a large expense in addition to the cost of euthanasia. Some breed organizations will provide financial assistance with the cost of a necropsy, so if you're considering this, check to see if assistance is available. Another consideration is the scheduling of a necropsy. It is very time-consuming to complete a necropsy involving sections of the spinal cord, brain tissue, or nerves—so you cannot wait until the last moment to schedule this. For many people, it's too painful to plan ahead for this, or your dog may be in crisis and you have to elect to let them go immediately. You may find, as I did, that your regular vet does not have the means to perform the necropsy. I felt very fortunate that I was able to eventually locate a vet who could do this, but this may not be an option for you. If you're fortunate enough to have your dog participating in one of the on-going clinical trials, a necropsy will be performed at time of euthanasia.

If you're able to overcome those factors and carry through with a necropsy, this is a selfless act that provides valuable information to the ongoing research into DM. But if you're unable to do this, for any of the reasons cited, or for your own personal reasons, do not question your decision. Just like choosing when to euthanize your dog, this is a very personal decision, and no one else can make it for you. Trust your heart, and do what you feel is most appropriate for you, your family, and your dog.

Veterinary Medical Diagnostic Laboratory Report

Mailing Address
PO Box 6023
Columbia, MO 65205

Location
810 E. Campus Loop
Columbia, MO 65211

Phone 573-882-6811
Web http://vmdl.missouri.edu

RDVM:
Dr Joan Coates

Clinic:
MU VHC Small Animal Research
900 E Campus Dr.
Columbia, MO 65211
Fax (573) 884-7563

Accession Number: 19-70029
Reference Number: DGF67
Case Coordinator: JOHNSON, GAYLE
Received: Feb 04, 2019
Finalized: Apr 19, 2019
Species: Canine
Sex: Female
Animal ID: Sassy Valere
Specimen: Fixed Tissue

Pathology

Patient Demographic Data
Comments   NONE

Pathology Comments
Comments

17 Apr 19: Examined is a specimen of spinal cord. The myelin staining is quite pale in all white matter tracts, with prominent penetratin blood vessels and vacuolation of axon sheaths, Dilated axon sheaths contai dilated axons or macrophages, besides being empty. There is a reduction in axons iwth increased homogeneous ground substance in dorsolateral funculi, Blood vessel in all funiculi have macrophages around them that are PAS-positive.The dura is irregularly thickened and spinal nerve roots have relatively small fibers with increased intervening stroma. Lipofusin is abundant in ventral horn neurons. The character of the ventral gray matter suggests that this is lumbar cord..
The peripheral white matter stains darkly for astroycte fibrillary cytoplasm with GFAP. Many gemistrpytes are evident in the dorsal and middle white matter. Almost no axons remain in the dorsal lateral tract, while large to small axons occur in other areas.

Severe DM

This report supersedes any previous reports issued for this case prior to 04/19/2019 at 2:38 PM
Accession Number: 19-70029
Status: Finalized

Friday, 19 Apr 2019 2:38 PM
Page 1 of 1

Necropsy results

Even though I was confident that Sassy had DM, the finality of seeing this report was like a punch in the gut. The last two words reduced me to tears.

Chapter Twenty-Four
Hope for the future

Despite the current bleak outlook of DM, there is hope on the horizon in the form of clinical trials being performed at universities across the country.

Finding the Cure for DM Foundation, Inc. (FCDMF) is an all-volunteer non-profit organization whose mission is to raise awareness about this disease, and to help fund research for treating, and ultimately, to find a cure for DM. Through their efforts, Project New Hope started in 2016 to evaluate a gene silencing technology.[11]

You can learn more about their work, or donate to their research funds, at **https://www.cure4dm.org/**

The Morris Animal Foundation has been supporting research about DM for almost thirty years, and is currently funding two studies.[12]

The important work started by FCDMF in Project New Hope is being continued at North Carolina State University, through the generous funding from a Morris Animal Foundation grant. DM is associated with a genetic mutation that causes a protein called superoxide dismutase (SOD1) to build up within nerve cells, eventually killing that cell. This study will evaluate a gene silencing treatment that prevents the build-up of SOD1.[13]

The Morris Animal Foundation is also funding researchers at Cornell University who are investigating whether an advanced MRI technique called diffusion tensor imaging, which can detect lesions on the spinal cords of humans, will result in a diagnostic tool that can reliably show if a dog actually has DM.[14] Early results of this research have been promising.

Clinical trials are taking place at the University of Missouri on a drug therapy to slow down the disease progression.[15]

Tufts University-Cummings Veterinary Medical Center has completed a study on gene silencing.[16]

All of these studies are advancing the body of knowledge about DM, and it's only a matter of time before breakthroughs occur that will either provide treatment options, better diagnostic tools, or both. Studies of DM are also benefiting research on human ALS, so this is important work.

Participating in the clinical trials at the University of Missouri has been a lot of things. We started in August 2016, and it's been scary, it's been heartbreaking, it's been promising, it's been joyous, it's been an emotional roller coaster. But, in the end it was all worth it. The dedication and compassion Dr. Coates and her team have to these dogs and the want/need to eliminate this disease is unsurpassed. I don't know that I've ever experienced anything like it before.

—*Jan Kump*
Lulu, Pembroke Welsh Corgi

Chapter 24 References

11. Finding the Cure for DM. (2017) "FCDMF: Project 'New Hope' 2017 Study Announcement." Accessed July 8, 2019 through https://www.cure4dm.org/2017%20Study%20Announcement_approved.pdf

12. Morris Animal Foundation. "Degenerative Myelopathy – Searching for Answers to a Debilitating Disease." Accessed July 10, 2019 through https://www.morrisanimalfoundation.org/article/degenerative-myelopathy-searching-answers-debilitating-disease

13. Morris Animal Foundation. "Ensuring the Safety of Novel Degenerative Myelopathy Therapy." Accessed July 10, 2019 through https://www.morrisanimalfoundation.org/study/ensuring-safety-novel-degenerative-myelopathy-therapy

14. Morris Animal Foundation. "Using Advanced Imaging to Diagnose and Monitor Spinal Cord Disease." Accessed July 10, 2019 through https://www.morrisanimalfoundation.org/study/using-advanced-imaging-diagnose-and-monitor-spinal-cord-disease

15. Veterinary Health Center, University of Miami. "Degenerative Myelopathy Clinical Trial." Accessed July 10, 2019 through https://vhc.missouri.edu/small-animal-hospital/neurology-neurosurgery/current-clinical-trials/

16. Rajewski, G. (2017). Cummings Veterinary Medicine. "Canine ALS: Lou Gehrig's patients could benefit from a Tufts study in dogs." Tufts University. Accessed July 10, 2019 through https://sites.tufts.edu/vetmag/spring-2017/canine-als/

Acknowledgments

The author would like to thank the following people for their support during Sassy's DM journey:

Utah Pet Rehab and Acupuncture, Dr. Tiffany Quilter, and Lauryn Narramore for your kind and loving care of Sassy for the eighteen months she was in hydrotherapy, and the home visits made to provide her with additional physical therapy. Sassy loved being with you.

Jenny and James Lowe, Jasmine Parker, Madison Briggs, Carrie Young, Boris Berganza, and Janet Schieving Larson from the local Utah Corgi group for your visits to Sassy, and for bringing her special treats during her last month. Your visits meant more to me than words can adequately express.

Dr. Scott Echols for your compassion on Sassy's last day, and for helping her cross to the other side. Your assistance in providing the necropsy for tissue donation was greatly appreciated.

The Pembroke Welsh Corgi Club of America (PWCCA) Charitable Trust for providing financial assistance for Sassy's necropsy.

Dr. Joan Coates, University of Missouri for your research and dedication to understanding this disease.

Bonnie Graham, Kathryn Everson, Deb Reid, Tina Kalinger, Bobbie Mayer, and Dr. Tiffany Quilter for your early critiques of this story, and your suggestions for improving it.

Madison Briggs for creating the cover design, along with formatting the book for publication. I could not have done this without your skills and assistance.

Many thanks to Mischa Safe Dziezyc, Dash-D Photography for taking time out of his busy schedule to take some photos of Sassy, and for generously allowing the use of one to be on the author bio.

To all the members of the Degenerative Awareness group, Corgis on Wheels, and #ShadeOutDM Facebook groups for their ongoing support and advice.

Michele Mukatis and John Cunningham for sharing the photo of the tracks in the snow that Hops made; Babs Rabenold for the photos of Biscuit knuckling; Joe Harre for his photos showing how DM dogs sit; and Madison Briggs for the photo of Sassy receiving fluids with a syringe.

Taylor Mietl (Lost Creek German Shepherds), and Kimberley Harvey (Dragsonsdale Corgis) for providing their perspective about breeding practices.

And finally, grateful thanks to my animal communicator Valerie, for providing so many check ins with Sassy and my other animals during this long journey. Without her ongoing support and communication with my animals, I would have been lost on a number of occasions.

Acknowledgments
In honor of the DM Dogs featured

I am grateful for the following people in the DM community for providing quotes and images to use throughout the book. Their honesty and vulnerability in sharing their personal journey with me touched my heart deeply: Tammy Diaz, Carly Lucas, Jan Salesky, Kirsten Nuffer, Pam Barnes, Jim Dolan, Angela Kalo, Deb Reid, Darlene D'Onofrio, Marisalena Manchego, Lauren Dill, Bonnie Kopp, Julie Georgiou, Chrissy Kiser, Jennifer Mulcahy, Clare Rosato and Gary Long, Lisa Slepetski, Meredith Casola, Michele Pierre, Nancy Northrop, Pamelia Brown, Denise Baker, Tauni Beckmann, Michele Mukatis, Babs Rabenold, Joe Harre, and Jan Kump.

Sammy

Kyle

Rookie

Tilly

Loki

Addison

Iris

Corbi

Minnie

Brodie

Zoey

Wesson

Maggie

Barney

Logan

Roxy

Hallie

Honey

Bailey

Rupert

KC

Denby

Teddy

Sasha

Lulu

Hops

Biscuit

Jasper Islington

Daisy

Fiona

Resources

To order a DNA test

Orthopedic Foundation for Animals
https://www.ofa.org

Author's Note: While there are other places to order the DM DNA test, the test results are not automatically added to the OFA database. I feel that if we are ever to have accurate numbers about how many dogs are affected by DM, the DNA results need to be in one place to provide that information. The OFA is dedicated to the mission of reducing the incidence of inherited diseases, and through their DNA repository, they are able to provide researchers with optimized family groups. To establish the DNA repository, the OFA has partnered with the Veterinary Genetics Lab at the University of California–Davis and the Animal Molecular Genetics Lab at the University of Missouri. If you choose to order your test kit through another company, please make sure that the DNA results are added to the OFA database.

To learn more about DM

Orthopedic Foundation for Animals
https://www.ofa.org/diseases/dna-tested-diseases/dm
Main website: **www.ofa.org**

Finding the Cure for DM Foundation
www.Cure4DM.org

DM Support groups on Facebook

Degenerative Myelopathy (DM) awareness group (for all dog breeds)
https://www.facebook.com/groups/DMDogs/

Corgis on Wheels (Pembroke and Cardigan Welsh Corgi breed specific)
https://www.facebook.com/CorgisOnWheels/

#ShadeOut DM (for all dog breeds)
https://www.facebook.com/groups/shadeoutdm.org/

Quality of Life Scale

Scout's House
http://scoutshouse.com/wp-content/uploads/2009/12/When-Is-It-Time3.pdf

Author's Note: The following is by no means an exhaustive list of all the companies that make handicapped pet supplies, nor is inclusion in this list an implied endorsement for the product(s) listed. If you are caring for a dog with DM, consult with your canine physical therapist or your veterinarian for recommendations. The real-world knowledge of people who have cared for a DM dog is invaluable, and there is a collective wealth of knowledge in the support groups on Facebook. Please consider joining those groups to ask questions on different products to determine if it will fit your needs. Be prepared for some trial and error–what works for one dog may not work for another.

Harnesses and slings

Help 'Em Up® Harness
https://helpemup.com

GingerLead
http://www.gingerlead.com

Flying Paws
https://flyingpaws.biz/

Cart makers

Eddie's Wheels
https://eddieswheels.com

K9 Carts East
http://www.k-9cart.com

K9 Carts West
https://www.k9carts.com

Walkin' Wheels
https://www.walkinwheels.com

No-Knuckling/Toe-Up Boot

Ortho Pets
https://orthopets.com/product/orthopets-toe-up-device/

Boots

PAWZ
https://www.pawzdogboots.com/
Available at most major pet supply stores or on Amazon

AllDogBoots.com
https://www.alldogboots.com/Orthopedic-Dog-Boots-s/2.htm

Ruffwear
https://ruffwear.com

Pet mobility resources

Handicapped Pets
https://www.handicappedpets.com/

www.ingramcontent.com/pod-product-compliance
Lightning Source LLC
Chambersburg PA
CBHW081426090426
42740CB00017B/3201